Ancient Okinawan
Martial Arts

....

Volume Two

KORYU UCHINADI

Compiled and Translated by
Patrick McCarthy and Yuriko McCarthy

TUTTLE PUBLISHING
BOSTON • RUTLAND, VT • TOKYO

First published in 1999 by Tuttle Publishing, an imprint of Periplus
Editions (HK) Ltd., with editorial offices at 153 Milk Street, Boston,
Massachusetts, 02109.

Library of Congress Cataloging-in-Publication Data

Ancient Okinawan martial arts : koryu uchinadi / written, compiled and
    translated by Patrick and Yuriko McCarthy. -- 1st ed.
      p. cm.
    Includes bibliographical references.
    ISBN 0-8048-3147-5 (pbk.)
    1. Martial arts--Japan--Okinawa-ken--History. I. McCarthy, Pat
(Patrick) II. McCarthy, Yuriko. III. Taira, Shinkin, 1897-1970.
Ryukyu kobudo taikan. English. IV. Miyagi, Chojun. Karatedo
gaisetsu. English. V. Title: Koryu uchinadi.
GV1100.77.A2A53 1999
796.8'0952'294--dc21   99-37846
                                                          CIP

                          Distributed by

USA   Japan
Tuttle Publishing   Tuttle Shokai Ltd
Distribution Center   1-21-13, Seki
Airport Industrial Park   Tama-ku, Kawasaki-shi
364 Innovation Drive   Kanagawa-ken 214-0022, Japan
North Clarendon, VT 05759-9436   Tel: (044) 833-0225
Tel: (802) 773-8930   Fax: (044) 822-0413
Tel: (800) 526-2778

Canada   Southeast Asia
Raincoast Books   Berkeley Books Pte Ltd
8680 Cambie Street   5 Little Road #08-01
Vancouver, British Columbia   Singapore 536983
V6P 6M9   Tel: (65) 280-1330
Tel: (604) 323-7100   Fax: (65) 280-6290
Fax: (604) 323-2600

        05 04 03 02 01 00 99   9 8 7 6 5 4 3 2 1

          Design by Northeastern Graphic Services, Inc.
            Printed in the United States of America

CONTENTS

Contents

Contents

Contents

FOREWORD

IT WAS THE FATHER of modern karate-do, Funakoshi Gichin, who once wrote, "by understanding the old we can come to better know the new." In realizing the value of that great man's words we may better appreciate just how important studying the history and philosophy of karate-do really is. Through learning about the past we may better prepare ourselves for understanding the present, and not repeat the mistakes of history. In addition, through understanding the past we may also better prepare ourselves for the future. It is knowing the value of this lesson that a message of greater importance makes itself apparent.

There has always been a need for a book of this magnitude: a book that reveals the wisdom of those who have come before us. As such, this text contains a myriad of never before published historical information and rare photographs, bringing you, the reader, closer to understanding the very evolution and meaning of karate-do.

This work presents the life story of Mabuni Kenwa, the founder of Shito-ryu karate-do. It is ironic that the history and contributions

Foreword

of one of the most brilliant innovators of modern karate-do has never been told before.

Miyagi Chojun's 1934 *Outline of Karate-do* is also presented here in its entirety, and as the only document to have been written by the founder of Goju-ryu, this presentation renders this work an invaluable collector's item.

Taira Shinken's 1964 *Ryukyu Kobudo Taikan* is also included in Vol. 1 in its entirety. A rare collector's item in Japanese, this English translation of Taira Sensei's only book renders the popular weapons traditions of Okinawa easier to understand. Never having been introduced to the Western world, this first English translation provides yet another reason why this work is such an important compilation.

In addition, included within Ancient Okinawan Martial Arts: *Koryu Uchinadi* are the minutes of the important 1936 meeting of the masters in Okinawa—a gathering that had a profound impact on the direction of modern karate-do.

The entire history of the Dai Nippon Butoku-kai (Japan's Emminent Association of Martial Virtues) and the impact it had upon the evolution of modern karate-do is also presented herein, further enhancing the value of this presentation.

Finally, a penetrating analysis of karate-do (its history, philosophy, and application) concludes this major volume.

Having spent nearly ten years in Japan, my research took me all over Asia and brought me into contact with many of the most prominent authorities of the fighting traditions. The analysis that lies before you, therefore, brings together a plethora of experiences and presents an untold story revealing the very principles upon which karate-do rests . . . and much more!

Through studying the past we are brought that much closer to understanding both the present and the future. Research of this nature is critical if we are ever to transcend the limitations of physical training, and so master the self. *Koryu Uchinadi* is a truly unique presentation, and one that will not only provide you with the answers you seek, but set you on a journey that may change your life.

Patrick McCarthy
Brisbane, 1999

1

Standing on the Shoulders of Giants: The Mabuni Kenwa Story

BY PATRICK MCCARTHY

"Compared to the fighting traditions of Japan's ancient samurai warrior, Mabuni's Shito-ryu must be to Okinawa's combative heritage what judo and kendo are to the classical schools of grappling and swordsmanship, ju-jutsu and ken-jutsu."

Introduction

Karate-do is the modern Japanese art of self-defense that fosters humility, pacifism, physical fitness, and spiritual harmony through physical discipline, philosophical assimilation, and protracted but methodical introspection. Once vigorously cultivated by Okinawa's feudal aristocracy, karate-do emerged from the synthesis of Chinese gongfu,[1] which was haphazardly introduced to the tiny island during Okinawa's old Ryukyu Kingdom, and a plebeian fighting method known as tegumi.

By nature, the island of Okinawa had evolved as a community of farmers and fishermen. However, because of its geographical location (between Japan and China, and not so far from the rest of

Asia), it ultimately became a bustling port for shipping and reshipping. Threatening the early part of this ascending prosperity, internal power struggles kept much of Okinawa contained in civil wars. To end the feudal conflict, a newly centralized government formed by King Shoshin (1477–1526) methodically prohibited the use and stockpiling of weapons in 1507. Powerful landowners were then forced to consider alternative means of protecting both themselves and their property. This ultimately led to the development of a native fighting discipline that introduced plebeian combative principles to a myriad of domestic weapon-usable objects.

Enjoying a protracted liaison with the Middle Kingdom (that is to say, mainland China), every facet of Okinawa's culture was deeply influenced by the more sophisticated Chinese culture. Up to and beyond the Meiji Restoration (1868), various kinds of quanfa had found its way across to this tiny archipelago, where the self-defense principles of Chinese quanfa enabled its users to subjugate an adversary without rendering serious injury unless absolutely necessary. Hence, such effective defensive principles were embraced as an adjunct to domestic law enforcement, and then more vigorously cultivated in a ritual of secrecy, especially after the military subjugation of Okinawa by the Satsuma samurai in 1609. Modern karate-do, representing varying interpretations of these Chinese defensive principles, evolved, for the most part, from these old disciplines.

These numerous interpretations have come about as each generation has produced innovators who have cultivated different yet equally effective ways for achieving karate-do's goal of perfection. Shito-ryu karate-do is one such interpretation. With an incredible repertoire of weapons, empty-hand kata (formal exercises), and a profound philosophical infrastructure, Shito-ryu karate-do has been described as the most comprehensive representation of Okinawa's ancient combative heritage.

In fact, when compared to the fighting traditions of Japan's ancient samurai warrior, Shito-ryu karate-do must then be to Okinawa's combative heritage what judo and kendo are to the classical schools of grappling and swordsmanship—ju-jutsu and ken-jutsu. The founder of the Shito-ryu tradition, Mabuni Kenwa (1889–1952), was one of Japan's most respected masters and pioneers of the Okinawan self-defense disciplines. Yet, the story of this unpretentious man and his efforts to establish a single style of karate-do remain virtually unknown.

Mabuni the Man

Mabuni Kenwa was one of the most gifted prodigies Ryukyu kempo Toudi-jutsu[2] in Okinawa during the dawn of this century. The seventeenth-generation descendant of a distinguished keimochi[3] named Oni Ougusuku, Mabuni Kenwa was born and raised in Okinawa's old castle district of Shuri. First schooled in the fighting traditions when just a boy, Kenwa was a weak and frail child, according to his 1938 book, *Kobo Kempo Karate-do Numon*. However, through karate-do training, his strength gradually increased as he matured into a powerful and, by all accounts, kind young man.

It was during the Itosu-Higashionna generation[4] of karate-do history that a young Kenwa Mabuni first began learning the mainstream traditions of Ryukyu kempo Toudi-jutsu. Thus did an insatiable curiosity instinctively bring him into contact with several other indigenous, albeit lesser-known, self-defense disciplines. These included tegumi (grappling) and various kinds of Kobudo such as bojutsu and sai-jutsu. The various interpretations (styles) we know today did not then exist in Okinawa, while the term karate-do had not yet been established.

The local self-defense disciplines were simply referred to in the Okinawan hogen (dialect) as *ti,* meaning hand(s), or Toudi, which literally translates to Chinese hand(s), while the Japanese renderings are *te* and To-te. (Te, meaning hand, is actually a generic term which implies Martial Arts.)

Indigenous fighting disciplines included self-defense traditions that had been cultivated in and around the old castle district of Shuri, much of which the legendary Bushi Matsumura (1809–1901) was responsible for handing down from his teacher, Toudi Sakugawa.[5]

The history of those self-defense methods has remained shrouded in folklore for as long as anybody can remember. Ironically, it was not until late 1926 that mainstream self-defense disciplines practiced in Okinawa were assigned such names as Shuri-te,

Naha-te, and Tomari-te. With a forthcoming visit by the dignified founder of judo, Dr. Kano Jigoro, this name change was done to eradicate karate-do's foreign (Chinese) image, and to thus associate the arts with the locality in which they were being cultivated. No one really knows how old the Naha-te, Shuri-te, and Tomari-te traditions were; however, with Kuninda (Naha's Kume village) being the former Chinese settlement on this one-time tributary state (est. 1393), most people assumed that quanfa had always been practiced there.

Notwithstanding, young Kenwa enjoyed a remarkable penchant for athletics, and was attracted to a myriad of native combative disciplines, excelling in all. In 1902, at just 13 years of age, Mabuni first started learning Toudi-jutsu directly under the eminent master Itosu Anko (1832–1915). Mabuni studied at the old master's home in Shuri, but later went on to learn from Hanashiro Chomo (1869–1945) while he (Mabuni) was a student at Okinawa's Prefectural First Middle School.

When Kenwa was twenty years of age and had already finished school, he trained directly under Higashionna Kanryo (the prominent master from Naha) thanks to an introduction from his good friend, Miyagi Chojun (1888–1953). That was in 1910, the same year that Miyagi Chojun was sent to Miyazaki Prefecture in Japan to serve his two-year compulsory military service.

Another *deshi* (personal disciple) of Higashionna Kanryo was Kiyoda Juhatsu (1886–1967) who had said that Mabuni had trained under Higashionna with an intensity he had not previously known. However, Mabuni's training under Higashionna Kanryo was cut short a year after it had begun, owing to his two-year military obligation for emperor and county.

Mabuni was one of only three men who had ever enjoyed the privilege of studying directly under two of karate-do's most important figureheads of that era, the other two students being Toyama Kanken (1888–1966) and Gusukuma Shimpan (1890–1954).

Receiving a personal introduction was the only way to receive instruction in the self-defense arts during those early days. Unlike today, where there are dojo (martial arts training halls) in practically every community and martial arts instruction is taken for granted, training took place as it had done for generations—beneath a strict veil of secrecy. It was not as if people were unaware of such practices, it was just that training had always been conducted in seclusion.

The *deshi* eagerly embraced a set of standards no longer fashionable to a generation so dominated by materialism. Sales gimmicks, two-for-one memberships, free one-week passes, and nineteen-year-old masters had not yet evolved. It was still considered an honor and a privilege to be accepted as a *deshi*. Also, the standard *dogi* (uniform) or dojo concept had yet to be established. The *deshi* usually trained outdoors in their *fundoshi* (loincloths, the standard underwear for that generation).

In 1913, nearing his twenty-third birthday, Mabuni began a career in civil law enforcement after completing his obligatory military service. This proved to be a valuable experience for him, especially after he was promoted and transferred to the Naha Central police station's detective division. As a detective, Mabuni traveled throughout the island, and so came into contact with a lot of individuals who were to have a profound influence upon him and his understanding of self-defense.

Mabuni Kenei says this of his father: "In his younger days, many would challenge my father to *kake-damashi* (a challenge-match, or an exchange of techniques) after they had heard that he was practicing *te*. These challenges he would accept, and would choose a quiet corner of town to serve as the venue. There were no special dojo like there are today, so we used to train and fight upon open ground. There was no street lighting, so we had to use lanterns, and in this dim light contestants fought. Each contestant would bring a 'second,' and after a period the second would intervene and stop the fight. They would then declare the winner, and the one who needed more training. Such challenges were often made to my father, and he frequently acted as a second for others."[6]

Mabuni Kenwa's position often brought him into contact with experts, and so he would eagerly seek their guidance. One such expert was Aragaki Seisho Tsuji Pechin (1840–1920),[7] a man whom both Itosu and Higashionna had described as being an eminent authority within the empty-hand and weapon disciplines. Seeking out this master of Monk Fist/White Crane quanfa at his home in Kuninda, Mabuni learned Sesoku bo-jutsu together with Niseishi and

Unsu kata that Aragaki had brought back from Fuzhou, Fujian. A former interpreter for the Ryukyuan court and pechin class kemochi, Aragaki also corrected the Sochin kata that Mabuni had learned from Master Itosu.

Although there is extensive speculation concerning Master Aragaki, the amount of factual information is actually quite small. Funakoshi Gichin (1827–1906) wrote that Aragaki had studied quanfa under Wai Xin Xian,[8] while Fujiwara Ryozo stated that in 1870 Aragaki Seisho had travelled to Beijing together with Zhao Xin (the last Chinese Sapposhi to visit the Ryukyu Kingdom).[9] Meanwhile, Nakaya Takao states that Aragaki had also accompanied Uechi Kanbum (1877–1948) and Matsuda Tokusaburo (1877–1931) upon their 1897 trip to China.[10] The son of Chitose Tsuyoshi (the founder of Chitoryu karate-do) recently informed me that his father had also studied briefly with Master Aragaki, while Toyama Kanken also wrote that he, too, had received instruction from the great master Aragaki. And lastly, we know that Aragaki was the first to teach Higashionna Kanryo before referring him to Master Kojo Taite (1837–1917).

Ochayagoten Celebration

On March 24th, 1867, a special ceremony was held at the Ochayagoten[11] of Shuri Castle's East Garden in Sakiyama village. This was to commemorate the visit of Zhao Xin, the last Sapposhi, to Okinawa in March, 1866.[12]

The program was divided into three parts: the *sanryuchu* (native folk dancing); the bujutsu (martial arts); and the *uchihanazutsumi* (drum music). This record of martial arts is now regarded as the "Ten Items of Bugei," and because it occurred during the old Ryukyu dynasty, it is thus regarded as an important document.

The Martial Arts Program

1. A demonstration of *tenbe* (shield and blade) by Maeda Chiku Pechin
2. A demonstration of bo-jutsu and sai-jutsu (pre-arranged sparring) by Maeda Chiku Pechin and Aragaki Tsuji Pechin

3. A demonstration of *jusanpo* (*seisan* kata) by Aragaki Tsuji Pechin
4. A demonstration of *bo* vs Toudi (pre-arranged sparring) by Maeda Chiku Pechin and Aragaki Tsuji Pechin
5. A demonstration of *chishaukiun* (small stick) by Aragaki Tsuji Pechin
6. Tenbe and bo-jutsu (pre-arranged sparring) by Tomura Chikudon Pechin and Aragaki Tsuji Pechin
7. A demonstration of *teshaku* (sai-jutsu kata) by Maeda Chiku Pechin
8. A demonstration of *kyusho jiaoshu* (Toudi-jutsu application principles) by Maeda Chiku Pechin and Aragaki Tsuji Pechin
9. A demonstration of Shabo (bo-jutsu kata) by Mr. Ikemiyagusuku Shusai (Shusai were Kume village *keimochi* [aristocratic] boys who would ultimately receive a government stipend in order to study in China, and later hold an official position in the service of the King).
10. demonstration of *suparinpei* kata by Tomura Chikudon Pechin

Mabuni was almost thirty-seven years of age before he established his first real dojo in October 1925. However, in the preceding years he had founded Toudi-jutsu clubs at the police department and at a local marine college. Of this remarkable man's many accomplishments, perhaps none was as noteworthy as his organization, together with his friend, Miyagi Chojun of the Okinawa Toudi Kenkyukai (The Chinese Martial Arts Research Society of Okinawa).

It was, in realizing that the interests they shared were far greater than the differences separating them, that informal gatherings headed by Motobu Choki's older half-brother (Motuba Choyu, 1865–1929) ultimately prompted Mabuni and Miyagi to organize an official Toudi-jutsu research society. Knowing that the task of researching, preserving, and promoting Toudi-jutsu was far beyond the reach of any one man, Mabuni and Miyagi, with Motubu Choyu's support, felt that by officially structuring their impromptu exchanges, the entire Toudi-jutsu movement could thus be elevated.

In many ways, this study group was Okinawa's first informal karate-do association—an early attempt at bringing together the loose-knit groups after the deaths of Itosu and Higashionna. Supported by local Toudi-jutsu practitioners, Mabuni Kenwa (with little space and next to no money) first established the Toudi-jutsu Kenkyukai at his Shuri home in 1918.

In a 1978 interview, Mabuni's first son, Kenei, remembered that when he was growing up, "everyone knew that the Mabuni house was a mecca for karate-do men."[13] Some of the most recognizable names supporting this study group were: Funakoshi Gichin (1868–1957, the principal student of Azato Anko); Matayoshi Shinko (1888–1947, an expert who had honed his skills in China); Yabiku Moden (1882–1945, a local weapons expert and a former student of Itosu); Oshiro Chojo (1887–1935, also a former student of Itosu and an instructor at the Okinawa Teachers College, but best remembered for his skill in the Yamane-ryu bo-jutsu of Chinen Shikiyanaka, 1780–1841); Chibana Choshin (1885–1969, also a former student of Itosu, who later opened his own club at Baron Nakajin's residence in 1919, and coined the term Shorin-ryu in order to describe his interpretation); Wu Xiangui (1886–1940, a Whooping Crane quanfa expert who immigrated from Fuzhou in 1912, and who is better known as Go Kenki); his friend Tang Daiji (1887–1937, an expert of Tiger Fist gongfu who immigrated from Fuzhou in 1915 and who is also known as To Daiki); Tokuda Anbun (1886–1945, another former student of Itosu who had also served as an instructor at the Teacher's College); Gusukuma Shimpan (1890–1954, a former student of Itosu and an instructor at the Okinawa Teachers College); Kiyoda Juhatsu (1886–1967, one of Higashionna Kanryo's most senior disciples, and the founder of Toon-ryu); Motobu Choyu (one of the island's most senior self-defense authorities); Hohan Sokon (1889–1982, the disciple of his uncle, Matsumura Nabe, the grandson of Bushi Matsumura who later founded Matsumura-ha Toudi [the Matsumura sect of Toudi-jutsu]); and Kyan Chotoku (1870–1945, a former student of both Matsumura and Itosu, and probably one of Okinawa's most popular self-defense teachers of that time).

The Kenkyukai presented many of the public demonstrations all over the island during that era, and with local connections within various bureaucratic, educational, and cultural organizations, the group was often called upon to give performances for visiting dignitaries. One year earlier (May 25, 1917) Funakoshi Gichin and Matayoshi Shinko (two of Mabuni's closest senior associates) went to Kyoto, where they demonstrated Toudi-jutsu at the Butokukai Butokusai (a martial arts virtues festival held at the Butokuden). This was the first demonstration of Toudi-jutsu to have ever been held on the Japanese mainland.

Of the many demonstrations that the Toudi-jutsu Kenkyukai gave perhaps none were as memorable as those given before members of the imperial family, including the Crown Prince (Hirohito) in 1921. Three of the most notable exhibitions of 1924 were as follows: the one held at the Taisho Theater in Naha that featured approximately forty participants and two that were held at the prefectural teachers' college gymnasium on the hill behind Shuri Castle, before and Imperial contigent from Tokyo, and later before Chichinomiya, himself.

Expanding the Okinawa Toudi Kenkyukai in an effort to accommodate the influx of his own students, Mabuni established a dojo in his backyard. That was in 1925. Because the Dai Nippon Butokukai had not yet officially recognized Toudi (as it had done judo and kendo), Mabuni, by law, had to report the new development to the local police station. Local government offices in Okinawa were, in fact, smaller representatives of the federal government, and so having the Okinawa Toudi Kenkyukai recognized by Okinawa Prefecture in actuality meant national recognition. In many ways, this was the first step to having Toudi recognized by the Butokukai's judo department.

If fate means preparation meeting opportunity, then perhaps the event that had the most effect upon Mabuni Kenwa's life was his 1927 demonstration before Dr. Kano Jigoro. With Kano planning to visit the island in October of that year, Okinawa Prefecture had decided to host a special welcoming celebration for him.

Gima Shinkin[14] wrote that Kano first visited Okinawa to lecture at the Okinawan Shihan Gakko (the Okinawa Teachers College), and then again four years later during the summer of 1926,[15] but during both trips he had never seen a Toudi-jutsu demonstration. Hence, as a part of the welcoming celebration, Mabuni and Miyagi were petitioned to organize a demonstration in his honor.[16]

In preparation for the celebration, the prefecture further recommended that the Toudi Kenkyukai consider using a term that might characterize Toudi as a martial tradition more closely associated with Okinawa, rather than the existing name which accented its Chinese origins.

In spite of Hanashiro Chomo having referred to Toudi as karate-do (empty hand) as early as 1905, everyone agreed that the names Shuri-te, Naha-te, and Tomari-te should be used to describe the Toudi that had been cultivated in and around the districts of Shuri, Naha, and Tomari. Gima Shinkin said that he had never heard Toudi-jutsu referred to as Shurite, Nahate, nor Tomarite before that time, and that it was Mabuni who had first told both Funakoshi and himself (Mabuni) about these terms when he and Miyagi visited Tokyo in 1928.[17]

Because it was organized by Okinawa's Board of Education, prefectural bureaucrats insisted upon a demonstration that reflected the *kata* (*pinan* and *naifuanchin*) that were being taught within the school system. As such, Mabuni was petitioned to provide a commentary on Shuri-te, while Miyagi would describe Naha-te. If there was any one man in Japan during that era who could influence the growth and direction of *budo,* then it was Dr. Kano, with his political pull, aristocratic connections, and International Olympic Committee recognition. It was for that very reason that Mabuni, frustrated by all the bureaucracy, believed that a demonstration of this nature would only impede the future direction of Toudi-jutsu rather than help it, and with that in mind, both he and Miyagi implored Kano to consider a private demonstration by the island's most senior experts the day after the school demonstration, to which Kano agreed.

The following morning, at the new Yudansha-kai dojo, Kano watched Yabu, Hanashiro, Kyan, Miyagi, and Mabuni perform *kata* and its application. Gima Shinkin wrote: "Mabuni told me that directly after the demonstration, Kano suggested that both Miyagi and I go to the mainland in order to introduce our disciplines there."[18]

Kano Jigoro arrived in Naha (Okinawa) on the third of January, 1927. For the next four days he visited the city office, a shrine, and a library. He visited Shuri, and then traveled as far northwards as Nago. Kano also gave seminars at the Naha Public Meeting Hall, and at the Elementary School Auditorium. These were attended by students from the Middle School, the Girls School, and the Teacher's College, together with members of the general public. Kano Sensei described seeing a demonstration of bo-jutsu and board breaking, as well as scrutinizing a presentation of Toudi.[19]

A pragmatic man, Mabuni was deeply influenced by the great Meiji period swordsman Yamaoka Tesshu (1836–1888), and often quoted him by saying: "Which do you think is better, the carpenter who needs the right tools to complete his task, or the one who can make do with what is available?" Brilliantly eclectic, Mabuni always made do with what he had. However, not very well-to-do financially, Mabuni was never able to pursue his lifelong ambition: to travel and study the fighting traditions in mainland China, as his teacher (Higashionna Kanryo) and friends had done. Nonetheless, in recognizing the importance of such a need, he did cultivate close friendships with Chinese quanfa experts Wu Xiangui (Go Kenki), Tang Daiji (To Daiki), and Uechi Kanbun. Wu and Tang had a major influence not only upon Mabuni but also his friends Miyagi, Kiyoda, and Matayoshi.

Mabuni's compulsion to understand the entire magnitude of kata ultimately provoked him to seek out, commit to memory, analyze, and then cross-reference almost every kata known to Okinawa. In addition to the "classical" Okinawan paradigms, Mabuni learned several gongfu *hsing* (kata) from Go Kenki, To Daiki, and Uechi Kanbun.

According to Fujiwara Ryozo, Mabuni Kenwa learned naifuanchin kata from a student of Matsumura Sokon named Matayoshi.[20] Later, when Mabuni demonstrated the kata for Itosu, his teacher, Itosu had said that it resembled the original form he had learned from a Chinese man named Channan in Tomari. However, in seeking to establish a standard everyone would follow, Itosu suggested that Mabuni practice the modern version.

Regarding Channan, some have said that he was a Zen monk, while others believe he was a former Qing dynasty (1644–1911) official. And still others suggest that he was a gongfu teacher who had fled China after the Boxer Rebellion in 1900. Perhaps he was all three! Whatever the case, it is said that Channan had left a secret book on gongfu with Itosu, a book that allegedly influenced him significantly. Some say that this book was the *Bubishi,* which Mabuni had hand-copied and then published in 1934. Others say that it was a copy of Qi Jiguan's 1561 *Ji Xiao Xin Shu,* a book from which came Itosu's idea for the *pinan kata.* However, no one can be sure because Channan's mysterious book has never surfaced.

Gima Shinkin also wrote that Funakoshi was so well known for teaching the *pinan kata* that many people referred to him as Pinan Sensei. Yet, it was Mabuni Kenwa who was the original master of *pinan,* not to mention the *hakutsuru kata,* the Kojo family fist kata, and the Five-Ancestor Fist kata.[21]

Another interesting, but little known, point about the *pinan kata* appears within the FAJKO (Federation of All-Japan Karate-do Organization) *Karate-do Directory.* Therein it is stated that "In 1919, at the age of fifty-one, Funakoshi Gichin, learned the *pinan kata* from Mabuni Kenwa."[22] That, of course, would make sense as Funakoshi Sensei (a student under Itosu) was primarily a student of Azato Anko (1827–1906) and had concluded his training with Itosu long before he established the *pinan kata* in 1905. After the turn of the century, it was Mabuni who became recognized as Itosu's foremost disciple.

Qinna

Little is written about Mabuni's relationship with Wu Xiangui and Tang Daiji. Kinjo Hiroshi[23] (a man described by Richard Kim as "a walking encyclopedia of karate-do history, philosophy, and application") believes that one of the principal reasons why Mabuni sought out their instruction, and that of Uechi Kanbum, may very well have been to gain a deeper understanding of qinna (literally, to seize and hold).[24] Often mistakenly referred to by the Okinawans as Tuidi-jutsu (digging into the cavities of the body unprotected by the skeletal structure), qinna represents the application principles of those techniques upon which kata initially unfolded. Culminated by his lengthy analysis of the *Bubishi,* the hallmark of Mabuni's Shito-ryu was his attention to kata application: the striking of anatomically vulnerable points (kyusho-jutsu); throws (nage-waza); the use of joint-locks, come-along techniques, and techniques of dislocation (kansetsu-waza), ground work (ne-waza); countering (gyaku waza); attacking the respiratory system (shime-waza) and grappling (Tegumi).

Before stylistic methods of gongfu were codified in China, qinna (as it later became known) served as the very first form of self-defense. A compilation of self-defense skills, qinna represented the principles of seizing and controlling an adversary without seriously injuring the adversary unless it was absolutely necessary. Because qinna has always been an effective deterrent in thwarting and controlling would-be attackers, it has served for centuries as a practical adjunct for peace officers at various levels of law enforcement.

In Toudi-jutsu (the Chinese eclectic-based self-defense disciplines that were once so vigorously cultivated within Okinawa's old Ryukyu Kingdom), this practice is referred to as *bunkai*—a generic term that describes and pertains to the analysis and application principles of kata. Modern Japanese karate-do has popularized other terms that nowadays describe specific components of *bunkai-jutsu,* for example: tori-te (tuidi in Hogan, which relates to seizing with one's hands); *kyusho-jutsu* (techniques that target vital points); *tegumi* (grappling hands); *kansetsu-waza* (joint-locks); *shime-waza* (strangulation techniques); and *atemi-waza* (a means of attacking vital points by way of techniques of impact).

In essence, qinna brings together all those principles of physical subjugation that have been cultivated throughout untold generations of practical experience, and often at the cost of human life. Qinna embraces the principles of:

- Twisting bones and locking joints
- Separating tendons from the bone (*fengin* or *zhuaging*)

- Seizing, manipulation, and/or striking of nerve plexuses (*dianxue*)
- Attacking the arteries (*duanmie*) and/or other anatomically vulnerable locations
- Respiratory (*bi chi*), blood, and air strangulations
- Organ-piercing blows (designed to shock organs not protected by the rib cage)
- How to rupture veins and arteries (blood-gate attacks)
- Grappling, takedowns, throws, ground work, counters, and escapes
- And combinations thereof

Qinna teaches one how to discourage an attack by hurting, incapacitating, or killing, if necessary. A shaolin precept and code of conduct handed down from ancient times that rationalized one's self-defense actions goes something like: "Avoid fighting at all costs. However, when no other choice is available, hurt rather than be hurt, maim rather than be maimed, kill rather than be killed." Qinna applications were never intended to be used within the arena or against well-trained warriors. Rather, qinna applications worked best against an attacker completely unaware of the methods being used against him. As such, applications represented practical responses against the habitual acts of physical violence that plagued the society in which they were brilliantly contrived, and they are continually perpetuated through kata.

The results of untold ordeals, each qinna principle was ingeniously contrived to neutralize an opponent's ability to attack through impeding motor performance, obstructing the air or blood flow, and rendering the attacker unconscious (or worse!) by attacking the adversary's vital-points.

Toudi-jutsu on Mainland Japan

Several historical accounts detail Toudi's early development and subsequent introduction to mainland Japan. For years, the Japan Karate Association had remained unchallenged in their campaign, leaving Funakoshi Gichin the patriarchal figure responsible for bringing this Okinawan phenomenon to the mainland. However, opposition maintains that Motobu Choki had been teaching on the mainland for more than a year prior to Funakoshi's arrival, while other reports describe several Okinawan students who were studying on the mainland and teaching Toudi long before the arrival of either Funakoshi or Motobu.

If there was ever any curiosity within mainland Japan concerning Toudi-jutsu prior to the efforts of Motobu, Funakoshi, and others, it had to have surfaced when the Imperial army first considered its value as an adjunct to physical training.

Impressed by the physical conditioning of several Okinawan conscripts during their medical examinations in 1891,[25] the army ultimately abandoned its interest in Toudi-jutsu because of its archaic training methods, poor organization, and the great length of time it took to gain proficiency. In short, such training could not adequately serve the needs of six- to eight-week boot camp training. However, that was not before a local campaign surfaced, the aim of which was to modernize its practice and purpose.

The movement, headed by Mabuni's principal teacher, Itosu Anko, was ultimately culminated in Toudi-jutsu becoming a part of the physical education curriculum of Okinawa's school system at the turn of the century. His 1908 address to the Education Ministry, a document now referred to as the "Ten Lessons of Itosu," clearly delineates Toudi-jutsu's aims and objectives.

Itosu's Ten Lessons[26]

Toudi did not descend from Buddhism or Confucianism. In the olden days, two Toudi schools (the Shorin and the Shorei[27] styles) were introduced from China. Both support sound principles, and it is vital that they be preserved and not altered. Therefore, I will mention here what one must know about Toudi.

1. Toudi does not only endeavor to discipline one's physique; if and when the necessity arises whereby one has to fight, Toudi provides the fortitude in which to risk one's own life in support of that effort. Toudi is not meant to be employed

15

against an adversary but rather as a means to avoid the use of one's hands and feet in the event of a potentially dangerous encounter.

2. Toudi's primary purpose is to strengthen the human muscles, thus making the physique as strong as iron and as hard as stone. One may then use the hands and feet as weapons—weapons such as the spear and halberd. In so doing, Toudi training cultivates bravery and valor in children and should, therefore, be encouraged within our elementary schools. Do not forget what the Duke of Wellington said after having defeated Emperor Napoleon: "Today's victory was first achieved from the discipline attained within the playgrounds of our elementary schools."

3. Toudi cannot be adequately learned in a short time. Like a torpid bull, regardless of how slowly it moves, it will eventually cover 1,000 miles; and so it is for the one who resolves to study diligently two or three hours each day. After three or four years of unremitting effort, one's body will undergo a great transformation, thus revealing Toudi's very essence.

4. One of the most important issues within Toudi is the training of the hands and feet. Therefore, one must always use the makiwara in order to develop them thoroughly. To do this effectively, lower the shoulders, open the lungs, and focus your energy. Grip the ground firmly in order to root your posture, and sink your ki—commonly referred to as one's life force or intrinsic force—into your tanden (just below the navel). Following this procedure, perform 100–200 tsuki (thrusts) each day with each hand.

5. One must maintain an upright position within the Toudi training postures. The back should be straight, loins pointing upward with the shoulders pulling downward, and a springiness should be maintained in the legs. Relax, and bring together the upper and lower parts of the body with the ki force focused in your tanden.

6. Handed down by word of mouth, Toudi comprises a myriad of techniques and corresponding meanings. Resolve to independently explore the context of these techniques, observing

the principles of torite (the theory of usage), and the practical applications will be more easily understood.

7. In Toudi training, one must determine whether the specific application is suitable for defense or for cultivating the body.

8. Intensity is an important issue for Toudi training. To visualize that one is actually engaged upon the battlefield during training does much to enhance progression. Therefore, the eyes should dispatch fierceness while the shoulders must be kept low; contract the body whenever lowering the shoulders and contract the body when blocking a strike or delivering a blow. Training in this spirit prepares one for actual combat.

9. The amount of training must be in proportion to one's reservoir of strength and condition. Excessive practice is harmful to one's body, and can be recognized when the face and eyes become red.

10. Toudi participants usually enjoy a long and healthy life thanks to the benefits of unremitting training. Practice strengthens muscle and bone, improves the digestive organs, and regulates blood circulation. Therefore, if the study of Toudi were introduced into our (athletic) curricula from elementary school, and practiced extensively, we could more easily produce men of immeasurable defense capabilities.

With these teachings in mind, it is my conviction that if the students at the Shihan Chugakko [the old name for the Okinawa's Teachers College] practice [Toudi] they could, after graduation, introduce Toudi at the local levels; namely in the elementary schools. In this way, Toudi could be disseminated throughout the entire nation and not only benefit people in general but also serve as an enormous asset to our military forces.

In modernizing karate-do, Itosu established a foundation upon which a new breed of teachers surfaced. While many of those first-generation teachers, like Funakoshi, Kyan, Yabu, and Hanashiro, had studied under the legendary Bushi Matsumura, Mabuni was among the few who had not.

Mabuni Goes to the Mainland

In 1928, and with Kano Jigoro's recommendation still fresh in his mind, a determined Mabuni Kenwa took an early retirement from the police department, gathered what little funds he had managed to save, and ventured northward to Tokyo with his good friend Miyagi Chojun. Visiting both Kano Jigoro and Funakoshi Gichin, Mabuni was able to demonstrate at the Kodokan, Tokyo Police Station, Tokyo University, and the Transportation Ministry. Thus did it soon became evident to Mabuni that Toudi-jutsu was, indeed, a growing trend that required men such as Miyagi and himself.

Meeting influential and anxious prodigies such as Konishi Yasuhiro (1893–1983, of Shindo Jinen-ryu) and Ohtsuka Hironori (1892–1982, of Wado-ryu karate-do ju-jutsu kempo), both Mabuni and Miyagi were invited to present lectures in and around the Kanto and Kansai regions. Well received in Osaka, and later in Kyoto at the Butokuden, Mabuni decided to establish his own following in the Osaka area out of respect for his good friend Funakoshi.

Mabuni established clubs within Osaka's west ward of Nari, and several universities where he ultimately built up a considerable following. Even to this day, Osaka is Japan's stronghold of Shito-ryn. Apparently, he was also quite instrumental in helping Miyagi establish his club at the Ritsumeikan University, where Yamaguchi Gogen of the Goju-kai first studied karate-do in 1931. In September 1932, Mabuni reinforced his base when, by popular demand, he organized the Toudi Kenkyu-kai at Kansai Gakuin University, and registered his dojo with the Dai Nippon Butoku-kai.

Despite this success and popularity, Mabuni was not a financially prosperous master of karate-do. Ohtsuka Hironori said that "Mabuni could have easily been a rich man several times over had he ever wanted to cash in on his popularity. He was liked by everyone, perhaps envied by some, but hated by no one."

Konishi Yasuhiro, who became Mabuni's closest friend within the mainland, wrote that Kenwa Sensei was so deeply committed to exploring the depths of Toudi-jutsu that he often spent what little money he had on research rather than food to feed himself and his family. Rarely was a moment of Mabuni's adult life far from karate-do; in fact, karate-do was his life! After Mabuni moved to Osaka, the Konishi's were like second parents to his son Kenei, who often stayed with them when his father was in the Tokyo area, teaching and lecturing.

On one occasion during the early Showa,[28] Konishi accompanied Mabuni south to Wakayama Prefecture where he met with Uechi Kanbum, after whom the Uechi system of karate-do was later named.[29] Uechi Kanbun had moved there, from Okinawa, together with his family, in 1924. Mabuni was intensely curious about what had kept his fellow islander in Fuzhou for so many years. Speaking about their trip, Konishi wrote in 1933 that Uechi Sensei could not speak Japanese very well, and lived like a recluse.[30] The kata Shimpa (mind wave) represents the defensive principles Mabuni learned from his meeting with Master Uechi. A simple and rare exercise, Shimpa features the basic grabbing and striking principles of both Fujian tiger boxing and Fujian dog boxing.

By 1933, due largely to the success of his teaching method, Mabuni had established a considerable reputation, along with an even stronger following, within the Kansai region. During what is now referred to as the era of great change in Toudi-jutsu, his style was referred to (by the Kansai people) as Hanko-ryu, meaning the half hard style, while supporters within the Kanto region simply called it Mabuni-ryu.[31] In April 1933, and with the blessings of Kano Jigoro, the Okinawan branch of the Dai Nippon Butoku-kai located in Naha officially admitted karate-do into their judo department under the name Toudi-jutsu. In December of the same year, and after meticulous efforts, Toudi-jutsu was finally ratified as a Japanese budo.

In 1934, Mabuni Sensei decided to designate his interpretation of Toudi-jutsu as Shito-ryu, naming it after his two principal teachers, Itosu and Higashionna. In 1939, Master Mabuni officially registered the name Shito-ryu with the Dai Nippon Butoku-kai.

Understanding the Name "Shito"

Comprised of two separate Chinese characters, *shi* and *to,* the term represents the first ideogram of the surname for Mabuni's two principal teachers, Itosu Anko and Higashionna Kanryo.

In the Japanese language, a single Chinese character (called *kanji*) often has more than one pronunciation. This grammatical phenomenon is referred to as the *on-yomi* (meaning the Chinese reading) and the *kun-yomi* (the Japanese reading). The *shi* of Shito, the *on-yomi* for the *kanji* meaning "thread" is normally read *ito,* as in the Okinawan surname Itosu. Similarly, *to,* the *on-yomi* for the *kanji* that means "east," is normally read *higashi.* This special combination represents Mabuni's intense regard for his two principle teachers. Although not the original name for his brain-child, it does reflect the very foundation upon which his style ascended, and subsequently became the orthodox name for his interpretation.

In 1927, Yabu Kentsu visited his son, Kenden, in Los Angeles and gave a demonstration of Toudi-jutsu at the American-Okinawan Club. En route to America, Yabu, also introduced Toudi-jutsu to Hawaii. Several years later, a growing popularity within Hawaii encouraged a local newspaper to invite more experts directly from Japan. Recognized as leading authorities of karate-do, Mabuni Kenwa, Funakoshi Gichin, and Miyagi Chojun were invited to Hawaii where they could each introduce their specific art to the Hawaiian people. This invitation was hosted by a Tokyo company on behalf of the Hawaiian Pacific Times Newspaper Company.

Because of the great time involved (traveling there, lecturing, teaching, and then returning to Japan), both Funakoshi and Mabuni were unable to make the trip. Therefore, despite his aversion to lengthy voyages, Miyagi Chojun traveled there alone in April 1934.

Nineteen thirty-four was a memorable year for Mabuni Kenwa as this was when he opened his Youshukan dojo in Osaka and met with remarkable success. One of Mabuni's most prolific disciples, Sakagami Ryusho (1915–1993), once mentioned that the name Youshukan was based upon the name of the school Master Mabuni had attended as a child.

Commanding such widespread respect within the karate-do community, Mabuni's reputation was equaled only by that of his colleague and friend Funakoshi; while Funakoshi was considered the principle force within the Kanto plain, Mabuni's jurisdiction was Okinawa and the Kansai region.

Kobudo

Although rarely mentioned, Mabuni was highly skilled in kobudo—the "old martial ways"; indigenous weapons traditions developed and handed down by Okinawans during feudal times.

Kobudo is a discipline that evolved primarily because weapons of war had been prohibited during Okinawa's early history. A lethal method of self-defense, Ryukyuan kobudo evolved through the application of combative principles to a myriad of domestic objects that were readily adaptable for use as weapons: horseshoes (*tekko*); millstone handles (*tuifa*); stone weights attached to lengths of rope (*suruchin*); boat oars (*eku*); the fishing gaff (*nunte*); sea turtle shells and machetes (*tenbi* and *rochin*); rice flails and the horse's bit and bridle (*nunchaku*); the hoe (*kuwa*); the six-foot wood cudgel (bo); the iron truncheon (sai); and garden sickles (*kama*) to name but a few of the more popular ones.

Being a policeman, it is no surprise to learn that Mabuni specialized in both sai-jutsu (the use of the iron truncheon) and bo-jutsu, the use of a wooden staff. These are two weapons traditions that were vigorously cultivated by Okinawa's *chikudon pechin kei-mochi*.[32] Although profoundly influenced by such weapons experts as Chinen Sanda (1842–1928).[33] Mabuni received most of his kobudo instruction from Chinen's best-known disciple, Yabiku Moden—a man who, like Mabuni, had also learned his Toudi-jutsu directly from Itosu.

In addition to his training with Aragaki, two other important kobudo experts with whom Mabuni also came into contact were Sueyoshi Jino (1846–1920) and Tawada Shimbuku (1851–1920), two individuals whose hard-earned reputations in sai and bo had won them great respect. From these two stalwarts Mabuni deepened his understanding of bo-jutsu and sai-jutsu while enhancing his kata repertoire.

Sought after not only for his knowledge of Toudi-jutsu, Mabuni Kenwa was often petitioned to teach kobudo. In fact, it was one of Funakoshi Gichin's most senior students, Taira Shinken (1897–1970), who benefited the most from Mabuni's teachings. Studying directly under Funakoshi Gichin from 1922, Taira began learning kobudo in 1929 from Yabiku Moden. In 1932, Taira moved to Gunma Prefecture, where he established his first dojo at the hot springs resort of Ikaho.

In February 1933, during a seminar at the Ikaho dojo, Yabiku Sensei awarded Taira with the shihan menkyo[34] and recommended that he further his study under Mabuni. In September of that same year, Master Funakoshi also traveled north to Ikaho, where he taught a seminar at Taira's dojo and assured Shinken Sensei that Master Mabuni would come to Gunma the next year. And sure enough, in 1934, Mabuni did travel north to Ikaho, where he presented a lecture on kobudo.

Taira was so taken with Mabuni's expertise that he petitioned the great master to continue his instruction. Master Mabuni taught Taira for six years. During that time, Mabuni taught Taira the bojutsu of Sueyoshi, Urazoe, and Sesoko. Taira also learned the saijutsu of Hamahiga and Hantaguwa from Master Mabuni.

Mabuni's genuine personality and profound knowledge of both karate-do and kobudo attracted a considerable following, many of whom came to support the independent kobudo movement upon which Taira later embarked. Among the most well known of Mabuni's students who helped to further Taira's kobudo campaign were Sakagami Ryusho (Itosu-ha), Kuniba Shyogo (Motobu-ha), Hayashi Teruo (Hayashi-ha), Konishi Yasuhiro (Shindo Jinen-ryu), and Mabuni's own son Kenei (Shito-kai). No less interesting to learn is the fact that their efforts were largely responsible for introducing and popularizing Taira's kobudo to the Western world—through their success as international teachers of Shito-ryu karate-do.

In the opening passage of Itosu Anko's 1908 "Ten Lessons," the great master wrote: "both (Shorin-ryu and Shorei-ryu) support sound principles, and it is vital that they be preserved and not altered." Misinterpreting Itosu's words, many people have concluded that the two styles should never have been combined. However, Master Mabuni understood that what Grandmaster Itosu actually meant was that it was only teaching methods that divided these styles, and that for each kata to be correctly preserved they had to be brought together to be analyzed. In doing so, Mabuni Kenwa ensured that each kata, a separate tradition unto itself, would never need to be altered.

Mabuni's eclectic Shito-ryu hybrid is characterized by a myriad of prominent paradigms (kata), most of whose individual histories have been lost in the annals of time. Having studied with Higashionna Kanryo for little more than a year, it was Kenwa's good friend Miyagi Chojun who kindly imparted what he had missed after he had gone into the military. Naturally, Shito-ryu's tensho kata also represents a part of what Mabuni Kenwa learned from its developer, Miyagi Chojun.

Miyagi said at the 1936 meeting of karate-do masters in Okinawa: "It is believed that karate-do has two separate sects: Shorin-ryu and Shorei-ryu. However, there is no clear evidence to support or deny this fact. If I was forced to distinguish the differences between these sects, then I would have to say that it is only the teaching methods that divides them."[35]

Another hallmark of Mabuni's Shito-ryu is the balanced way in which he used pliability and power. This synthesis also extended to Mabuni's personality, and perhaps explains why he was able to yield in the winds of adversity. Regardless of how one cares to remember him, Mabuni Kenwa was able to preserve and carry on an exemplary friendship with many of those that could not all stand to be in the same room. Another example of Mabuni's genius can be observed by way of his five principles of blocking:

1. *Rakka* (dropping flower): intercepting an attack by dropping down onto it with such force, that if it was a tree being struck all the leaves or flowers would fall from its branches.
2. *Ryu shui* (running water): the ability to respond to changing conditions with circular movement, in the same way that flowing water naturally conforms to its path.
3. *Kusshin* (up and down): using vertical movement in order to subjugate an adversary.
4. *Teni* (changing position): three principles: initiative, combative engagement distance (*ma-ai*), and the space between oneself and an opponent necessary for subjugation by shifting and pivoting (*tai-sabaki*).

5. *Hangeki* (countering): the principles of brief but intelligent responses; also encompasses the capacity to overcome an adversary with or without physical confrontation.

Opposition

At one time, a rumor surfaced within karate-do's competitive world suggesting that Mabuni Sensei only knew kata and did not advocate sport fighting. In reality, the comment is a great compliment, although the allegation, coming from young competitive fighters who had little or no respect for kata, was intended to ridicule Mabuni.

Yet nothing could have been farther from the truth! Like Motobu Choki, Ohtsuka Hironori, Kudaka Kori (1907–1988), Sawayama Masaru (1906–1977), and Yamada Tatsuo (1905–1967), Mabuni was one of the very few men to pioneer contact fighting and protective equipment in competition.

In a 1989 interview with Sakagami Ryusho (one of Mabuni's most prolific disciples), Sakagami described the former Okinawan policeman as a mild-mannered gentleman who had tasted his fair share of street encounters while in law enforcement. His son, Mabuni Kenei, said that his father often told him how his karate-do had helped him as a street cop.

Mabuni maintained that karate-do was never intended to be used within an arena against other trained athletes. He described *kumite* as a completely detached entity that had surfaced when karate-do became a cultural recreation influenced not only by kendo and judo but by the younger generation within the highly competitive university karate-do clubs. Mabuni had never liked competitive fighting, saying that it always seemed to bring out the worst in human behavior, but that it did have some good points. About this very same issue Shoshin Nagamine wrote:

> I don't mean to suggest that I have a totally negative opinion about karate-do's competitive element, it's just that I feel that it is too shallow. Regardless of whether it is Okinawa, the Japanese mainland, or the world in general, *jiu-kumite* (free-sparring) ignores the principles to which kata apply. Simply put, *jiu-kumite*

should reflect the kata, because kata is the origin of karate-do. If there is no kata, it is not karate-do, just kicking and punching.[36]

Having also learned from Mabuni, both Ohtsuka Hironori and Konishi Yasuhiro described him as a warm and calm person whose kind and charitable character was indicative of Yamaoka Tesshu, the man who Mabuni so revered. Kinko Hiroshi told me that until the day that Mabuni died, almost everyone regarded him (Mabuni) as the guru of karate-do.

Whenever someone needed to learn new kata, make necessary corrections, or analyze its applications, they went to Mabuni. "And that included Funakoshi," concluded Kinjo Sensei. Ohtsuka Sensei, who had been deeply influenced by Mabuni, said that many of Funakoshi Sensei's kata either came directly from Mabuni or were corrected by him. Regarded by the Nihon Karate Kyo-kai (the JKA) as the father of modern Japanese karate-do, Funakoshi Gichin spoke highly of Mabuni Kenwa and visited Mabuni in Kansai, bringing with him his top students to learn and study new kata.

The Dai Nippon Butoku-kai

Responsible for regulating and supervising all the martial arts throughout the entire country, from the post-Edo period until the end of World War II, was the distinguished Dai Nippon Butoku-kai. Representing centuries of illustrious cultural heritage, the Butoku-kai's ultratraditional bugei and budo cliques were deeply concerned with Toudi-jutsu's growth and direction, and the hostilities openly vented between rival leaders.[37]

This, coupled with the disorganized teaching curricula, the lack of social decorum, and the absence of formal practice apparel, compelled the Butokukai to regard the escalating situation as detrimental to Toudi-jutsu's growth and direction upon the mainland, and so set forth to resolve it.

The principal concern focused not only upon ensuring that Toudi teachers were fully qualified to teach but that the teachers actually understood what they were teaching. For Toudi-jutsu to be accepted within mainland Japan called for the development and implementation of a unified teaching curricula, the adoption of a standard practice uniform, a consistent standard for accurately evaluating the various grades of proficiency, the implementation of Kano Jigoro's dan-kyu system, and the development of a safe competitive format through which participants could test their skills and spirit.

Just as twelve inches always equals one foot, the Butoku-kai's intention was to establish a universal set of standards, as had been done with judo and kendo. This was also a goal that Master Mabuni fully supported.

No less demanding were the powerful forces of nationalism combined with anti-Chinese sentiment, and together did they compel the Toudi-jutsu movement to reconsider a more appropriate ideogram to represent their discipline. So, rather than maintain the current China-linked ideogram, there was pressure applied for the adoption of the Japanese pronunciation of *kanji*. Hence, karate-do instead of Toudi. In making the transition, the Ryukyu kempo Toudi-jutsu movement would also abandon the *jutsu*[38] suffix and replace it with the modern term *do,* as in judo and kendo.

The wearing of sashes or belts was an idea conceived by the late founder of judo, Kano Jigoro, and this idea was adopted by the karate-do movement. Kano foresaw the need to distinguish the difference between the advanced practitioner and the different levels of beginners, and so he developed the dan/kyu system. The dan, or black belt, indicated an advanced proficiency level, and those who earned it became known as *yudansha* (dan recipients); while the kyu degrees represented the varying levels of competency below the dan, and were known as *mudansha* (those not yet having received dan ranking).

Kano Sensei felt it particularly important for all students to fully realize that one's training was in no way complete simply because one had achieved the dan rank. On the contrary, he emphasized that the attainment of the dan merely symbolized the real beginning of one's journey. By reaching black belt level, one had, in fact, completed only the necessary requirements to embark upon a relentless journey without distance that would ultimately result in self-mastery.

The Butoku-kai also conceived of and issued the first distinguished titles for the modern budoka who were considered outstanding in their particular disciplines. The Dai Nippon Butoku-kai's budo ranking system was, and still is, the evaluation of an individual's progress toward the attainment of human perfection through the practice of the fighting traditions. This evaluation is not based solely upon physical prowess, but rather encompasses one's entire physical, moral, and spiritual development: budo's goal of cultivating our world-within in an effort to enhance the world-without. Promotions issued by the Dai Nippon Butoku-kai were, and still are, based upon this standard.

The first *shihan* (master teacher) titles were: *hanshi* (which indicates a model expert or teacher by example) and *kyoshi*. Originally called *tasshi,* this translates into English as a teaching expert. In 1934, the title *renshi* was introduced. This suggests a well-trained or skilled expert, and even to this day the Butoku-kai continues to issue these titles.

It may seem rather ironic that Konishi Yasuhiro, a man who had learned from Motobu Choki, Funakoshi, Miyagi Chojun, and Mabuni Kenwa, would be the one in charge of issuing rank certification to those who had taught him! However, in 1938, the Butoku-kai made him chairman of the committee responsible for issuing karate-do teacher's licenses through the judo section. The move was supported by most *karateka,* but did not sit well with everyone, especially Funakoshi and Miyagi.

Funakoshi called it blasphemy, yet went on to receive his teacher's license from the Butoku-kai. Regarding Konishi's Butoku-kai position, Mabuni said: "All one need do is evaluate his pivotal contributions: he holds a prominent position within the budo world, he is highly regarded as a kendo teacher, a respected ju-jutsu enthusiast, a man of wealth and position, and his efforts are having quite an influence upon the growth and development of modern karate-do, despite Funakoshi's protestations."

Some of the most recognizable karate-do teachers to receive the prestigious Butoku-kai titles have been: Mabuni Kenwa (Shito-ryu); Miyagi Chojun (Goju-ryu); Funakoshi Gichin and his son Gigo (Shotokan); Konishi Yasuhiro (Shindo Jinen-ryu); Ohtsuka Hironori (Wado-ryu); Yamaguchi Gogen (Goju-kai); Nagamine Shoshin (Matsubayashi-ryu); Shinzato Jinan (Goju-ryu); Izumigawa Kanki (Goju-ryu); Higa Seiko (Goju-ryu); Yagi Meitoku (Goju-ryu); Ueshima Sannosuke (Kushin-ryu); Kinjo Hiroshi (Koryu Uchinadi); and Sakagami Ryusho (Itosu-kai Shito-ryu).

In May 1938 (the same year Mabuni Sensei became a standing member of Konishi's Ryobu-kai karate-do organization), the karate-do movement was officially authorized to give group demonstrations at the Butoku-sai—the Dai Nippon Butoku-kai's annual budo festival held at the Kyoto Butokuden on Boys Day (May 5). On May 5–6, 1940, at the forty-fourth annual Kyoto Butokusai, demonstrations of each karate-do ryuha were publicly presented for the first time. (This year's festival had been special, for it had commemorated the year 2600 in Japanese history.)

Mabuni the Author

If Mabuni Kenwa's name is not as well known as his friend Funakoshi Gichin, then his outstanding literary contributions have to be even less well known. This was due to the fact that that his books were already out of print before the war, and were never translated into English. Now, however, more than half a century later, the magnitude of his research is resurfacing as his books are being republished.

Among the several books he authored, Master Mabuni was the very first karate-do teacher to bring the secret Fujian treatise on gongfu, the *Bubishi,*[39] into the open. In 1934, Mabuni Sensei made this secret document public and wrote: "On the recommendation of my colleagues, I am presenting this work so that others may benefit."

Mabuni Sensei noted that he had made a copy of the old manual from a copy of an old Chinese book on gongfu that his venerated teacher, Master Itosu, had himself duplicated. He said: "I have used the *Bubishi* in my research, and secretly treasured it." Included with his study of *seipai kata,* the *Bubishi* is an ancient manual of Chinese gongfu that unravels the mysteries surrounding the evolution of karate-do, and reveals its connection to Fujian white crane gongfu and monk-fist boxing.

Disclosing the *kata happoren* (*paipuren*), *nepai* (*nipaipo*), and *rakkaken,* the *Bubishi* also includes a myriad of self-defense techniques, application principles, a hoard of herbal remedies for trauma-related injuries, and the original ideals that once governed the behavior of those who mastered these secrets.

Philosophically, the *Bubishi* is as important to karate-do as Sun Zi's *Art of War* and Miyamoto Musashi's *Book of Five Rings* are to the art of strategy. Politically, it is as vital to the leader of karate as is Machiavelli's *The Prince.* By comparing some of the text of Funakoshi Gichin's 1922 *Ryuky Kempo Toudi-jutsu,* the 1925 reprint entitled *Rentan Goshin jutsu,* and the 1935 publication *Karate-do Kyohan,* we can see how he, himself, was influenced by the *Bubishi,* while Higashionna Kanryo also revered this Chinese document. The disciple of Higashionna, Miyagi Chojun, also considered this text very special, referring to it as "The Bible of Karate-do." Indeed, Miyagi selected the name of his style, Goju, from a passage he had found within this ancient text, and used this to express and represent his own unique tradition.

The *Bubishi* also served well Shimabukuro Tatsuo (1908–1975) when he established the moral guidelines for his Isshin-ryu karate-do tradition. The *Bubishi* had such a profound affect upon Yamaguchi "the Cat" Gogen (1909–1989) that he, too, publicly referred to it as his "most treasured text."

In his efforts to provide a deeper understanding of the self-defense disciplines, Mabuni published a number of his own works. These included his first book, *Karate-jutsu,* which was published in 1933.[40] Most regrettably, this volume remains untraceable. Another of his works was *Kobo Jizai Goshin-jutsu Karate-do Kempo,* and this he published the following year, on March 5, 1934. One hundred and fifty-three pages in length, and featuring the theory and application of two kata (*sanchin* and *seiunchin*), this book sold for 1.20 yen.

Another book authored by Mabuni was *Seipai no Kenkyu Goshijutsu Hiden Karate-do Kempo.* Published on October 8, 1934, this volume comprised 176 pages, sold for 1.50 yen, and included the *Bubishi.* The second edition of this book was published later that month, on October 25, and was retitled *Kobojizai Karate-do Kempo and the Study of Seipai.*

The following year, on October 10, Mabuni Sensei published his

Karate-do Numon. This contained 210 pages, and sold for 1.80 yen. Considered his best work of all, this volume was rereleased three years later, on March 25, 1938, under the title *Kobo Kempo Karate-do Numon.* Published with the assistance of Nakasone Genwa, this was an exposition of Mabuni's personal research and was considered by one writer to be the real "Master Text" of karate-do. Addressing the entire spectrum of karate-do, Mabuni Kenwa won widespread recognition during that prewar era with this book and, considering the magnitude of this work, it is surprising to hear that it has never been translated into English.

Nakasone Genwa (1886–1978) was a broad-minded graduate from the Okinawa Teachers College. Relocating to Tokyo, he learned karate-do from Toyama Kanken at Toyama Sensei's Shudokan dojo.[41] There, he involved himself with Japan's socialist movement and, ultimately, served as the publisher of its newspaper.

In 1934, he began to support and publish several books on karate-do. Nakasone's best-known work is the 1938 *Karate-do Taikan* (Encyclopedia of Karate-do), which, in addition to Funakoshi Gichin, Hanashiro Chomo, Ohtsuka Hironori, Gusukuma Shimpan, and Chibana Choshin, features Mabuni Kenwa performing Aragaki's *sochin kata.*

Nakasone is probably best remembered for organizing the "Meeting of the Masters," sponsored in part by Ota Chofu, editor of the *Ryukyu Shimpo* newspaper in 1936.[42] After the war, Nakasone continued a career in politics, and in 1973 authored *From Okinawa to Ryukyu.*

Mabuni Sensei also appeared within Konishi Yasuhiro's publication *Karate Jotatsuho* (How to Master Karate), where he illustrated the *patsai* (*bassai*) *kata.* Kinjo Hiroshi told this writer that Mabuni was, in fact, terribly envied by rival karate-do teachers when he was alive simply because of how much he knew. Master Kinjo maintains that Mabuni's research and understanding of the fighting traditions put him in a category all by himself. According to Kinjo Hiroshi, that served as the basis from which several unkind rumors came from the sport faction, by those who had little interest in kata, or karate-do's historical or philosophical elements.

In an advertisement that he ran in his book on *seipai,* Mabuni describes himself as a *shihan* of Goju-ryu[43] kempo, teaching Japanese kempo karate-do-jutsu. Promoting his dojo in Osaka, he stated in writing that karate-do is a great way to get in shape and add years to one's life. It is an effective form of self-defense, and an idealistic training method that requires no special equipment or practice place. Moreover, there is no risk in learning and no restrictions upon age or sex. Anyone can learn, and it does not take too long when compared to other kinds of budo.

Within his book are a number of endorsements from newspapers, noted authorities, and friends supporting the forthcoming publication of *Kobo Jizai Goshin-jutsu Karate-do Kempo*. Funakoshi recommended the book by saying: "Mabuni Kenwa is my good friend and a remarkable karate-do researcher. Currently regarded as the leading expert, Mabuni Sensei has been collecting a myriad of research materials for a very long time, and is unsurpassed among others because of his mastery of so many kata."

During his January 1927 visit to Okinawa, where he observed two days of demonstrations, Kano Jigoro encouraged Mabuni to introduce his karate-do throughout Japan.

Konishi Yasuhiro said: "My friend Mabuni Kenwa has released this new book at just the right time. His book provides instruction and brings a freshness to an art that was in danger of disappearing from the budo world. I believe that Mr. Mabuni's book will be a great asset in helping improve the physical fitness of the Japanese people. An interesting publication that you simply won't want to put down once you start reading it, Mabuni's book is well written, easy to understand, and clearly detailed."

The *Osaka Mainichi* newspaper wrote: "The author is a well-known master who explains the essence of karate-do kempo. This publication contains numerous photographs and illustrations."

The *Hokushi Mainichi* newspaper wrote: "Because of the times we all face, everyone should read this book by Mabuni Kenwa. It is easy to understand and well illustrated."

The *Chogoku Minpoo* wrote: "A long time ago, Bodhidharma taught quanfa to his students as a means of improving their health. This method brought together the physical and spiritual and, later, found its way across to the Ryukyus where, affected by indigenous cultural forces, it was further cultivated."

"Once a secret practice, karate-do has now been introduced into many local areas. Mabuni Sensei's book is ideal for learning self-defense, improving one's general health at the same time. Learning karate-do does not require much time or money, and one can practice either by oneself or in a group."

The *Otaru* newspaper wrote: "Karate-jutsu is suitable for the times in which we now live. With karate-do fever widespread, it has since been introduced all over the country. Karate-do-jutsu appeals to everyone because it has no restrictions upon age or sex. It is easy to learn and very effective. Written by the great Goju-ryu karate-do kempo master Mabuni Kenwa (who teaches at locations such as Kansai University), this book explains karate-do in detail, is well illustrated, and easy to read. This book is the result of many years of research, and reflects his great mastery."

Mabuni had also planned to publish a book on women's self-defense titled *Mabuni-ryu Karate-do Kempo Joshi Goshin-jutsu*. In that book he was going to address the different ways in which women should study karate-do for self-defense, with which he had spent a lot of time and effort attempting to establish. The *kata aoyagi* (green willow) and *myojo* (Venus) represented Mabuni's unique self-defense applications developed specifically for women with or without detailed experience in karate-do.

In an advertisement promoting this book, Mabuni wrote that schoolgirls, housewives, ladies, and career women, regardless of age, could acquire defensive skills by learning to be like the green willow (*aoyagi*) in a powerful wind (yielding to overcome) and in so doing retain and maintain their virtue. Japanese women generally stop exercising when they finish their schooling, and Mabuni wanted them to understand that inactivity contributed directly to health problems, and that by practicing karate-do, women could not only learn to defend themselves but improve their health at the same time.

Another book he had planned to write was *Goju-ryu Karate-do Kempo, Sochin and Kururunfa*. The advertisement for this book stated that the *sochin* and *kururunfa kata* included techniques not found in other kata, such as reverse grabbing techniques, special throws, and reverse head-butts to the solar plexus.

Among the many things that Mabuni Kenwa wrote were two

interesting pieces for a local Okinawan tabloid. In one article, he addressed the importance of health and spiritualism, and described karate-do as an ideal vehicle. That article, entitled "Budo for Life," appeared in the March 1941 *Culture Okinawa Monthly* magazine. The other, which appeared in the May issue of the same magazine, addressed the need to unify karate-do, and was entitled "Establishing Karate-do as a Single Sect of Japanese Bushido." Together, these compositions clearly illustrate how Mabuni imagined the future direction of karate-do.

Transcending the Boundaries of Physical Training

Mabuni felt that the ultimate aim of the fighting traditions was: to recognize and overcome the real enemy (the enemy within), to go beyond the impulse of fighting with others, to transcend ego-related distractions, and to bring man back into harmony with nature through austerity, philosophical study, and protracted introspection. Kinjo Hiroshi told me that one thing that impressed him more than anything else about Master Mabuni was when he said: "There are no styles of karate-do, just varying interpretations of its principles. Those who master karate understand the importance of cooperating with the infinite rather than continuing to resist the inevitable. Karate-do can enhance the value of life itself. People seem to place too much emphasis upon this style or that style, this teacher or that teacher, winning and losing. This has nothing to do with karate-do's ultimate aim. Living in the past is as foolish as thinking we can travel to the future; there is only this moment in life. We must all learn to enjoy the beauty of the moment without prejudice, even if it requires a lifetime of study, this is the beauty of karate-do. The answers can only be found within, and those who have truly found the answers need never look anywhere else."

The *do* of karate-do merely describes the spiritual path upon which followers of karate-do travel en route to the world within: to the inner discovery. What else can the *do* of karate-do represent if not the Dao? An ancient proverb describing the Way reads: "Although there are many paths that lead up a mountain, there is only one moon to be seen by all those who reach its summit."

A staunch advocate of the moral values established to govern the behavior of karate-do practitioners, Mabuni concluded that understanding the deepest meaning of karate-do first meant transcending ego-related distractions and finding inner peace. In an abstract poem, Mabuni Sensei wrote that "When the spirit of karate-do [the *bu* of budo] is deeply embraced, it becomes the vehicle [described as a boat] in which one is ferried across the great void (one's mind) in order to discover the purpose or meaning of life [described as paradise island; see poem].

Conclusion

In spite of the Butokukai's plans for unifying karate-do being abandoned during the postwar depression, Mabuni Kenwa's contributions to the discipline's development remain unparalleled. Having sought out and studied under the most eminent masters of his time, forging a remarkable tradition, producing a number of prolific students, and publishing several outstanding works on the discipline, Mabuni Kenwa's contributions to the development of modern karate-do have, like a tall tree deep within the vast forest, remained largely unknown. They have, nonetheless, profoundly influenced the evolution of modern karate-do. A genius is rarely acknowledged during his or her own lifetime, but if there is any truth in the expression "tall trees provoke the pride of the winds," then Mabuni Kenwa was unquestionably the tallest tree within the forest of karate-do.

Yet, having said that, it was not the magnitude of this man's knowledge that set him apart from the others but the application of that experience, and a gift for transforming his vision into a valuable tradition benefiting all karate-do, that made Mabuni Kenwa such a remarkable human being. Anybody can learn to kick and punch; getting beyond ego-related distractions while navigating the turbulent rivers of one's life, with self-dignity and respect for others . . . this is the legacy Mabuni left to all followers of karate-do.

Grandmaster Mabuni Kenwa died in 1952 at the relatively young age of sixty-three. Leaving behind a legacy of knowledge so deep and penetrating that even to this day the magnitude of his research has yet to be completely evaluated or fully understood. In leaving this world, this remarkable man's contributions remain intact, waiting to be discovered by all those who practice Shito-ryu karate-do. If Mabuni Kenwa was able to see any farther than others, it was only by standing upon the shoulders of giants. Nothing of any value is ever gained without humility, diligence, and the guidance of others.

Mabuni Kenwa's Karate-do Genealogy

Principal Teachers

Itosu Anko
(1832–1915)
Shuri Shaolin

Higashionna Kanryo
(1853–1917)
Kume Shaolin

Hanashiro Chomo
(1869–1945)
Shuri Shaolin

Wu Xiangui
"Go Kenki"
(1886–1940)
Fujian Crane

Aragaki Seisho
Tsuji Pechin
(1840–1920)
Kume Shaolin

Sueyoshi Jino
(1846–1920)
bo-jutsu

Tawada Shimbuku
(1851–1920)
sai-jutsu

Yabiku Moden
(1882–1945)
bo- and sai-jutsu

Mabuni Kenwa
(1889–1952)
Shito-ryu
founder

Principal Students

Taira Shinken
(1897–1970)
Ryukyu kobudo

Iwata Manzo
(1924–1992)
Shitokai

Mabuni Kenei
(first son)
(1918–)
Shito-ryu

Mabuni Kenzo
(second son)
(1927–)
Shito-ryu

Konishi Yasuhiro
(1893–1983)
Shindo Jinen-ryu
    Seishikai

Sakagami Ryusho
(1915–1993)
Itosukai

Kokuba Kosei
(1901–1958)
Motobu-ha

Tani Chojiroh
(1921–)
Taniha Shukokai

Uechi Kanei
(1904–1993)
Shito-ryu kempo

Sawayama Masaru
(1906–1977)
Nihon Kempo

Hayashi Teruo
(1924–)

Seiki Hiroshi
Shudokai
Hayashi-ha

Fujitani Masatoshi
Meibukai

Fuji Kozo
Shingikai

Abe Iwao
Doshikai

Takayama Teruo
Kenseikai

Tomoyori Ryusei
(1909–1977)
Kenyukai

Kimura Kempe
Nambukai

Watanabe Masaru
Seikikai

Shitoryu Karate-do Kata

Itosuha
(Shuri Shaolin)
Pinan 1–5
Naifuanchin 1–3
Jitte
Jion
Jiin
Bassai sho
Bassai dai
Kusanku sho
Gojushihou
Chinto
Kusanku dai
Shiho-Kusanku
Chinte
Rohai 1–3
Kuniyoshi Kusanku

(Tomari Shaolin)
Wankan
Matsumora Rohai
Wanshu
Wanduan (Wando)
Tomari Bassai
Tomari Chinto

Higashionnaha
(Naha Shaolin)
Sanchin
Suparinpei
Seisan
Seipai
Seiunchin
Saifua
Kururunfa

Miyagiha
(Naha Shaolin)
Tensho
Gekkisaidai-ichi
Gekkisaidai-ni

Go Kenkiha
(Fujian Crane Gongfu)
Happoren (Paipuren)
Nepai (Nipaipo)
Hakutsuru

Ishimineha
(Shuri Shaolin)
Ishimine Bassai

Aragakiha
(Kume Shaolin)
Unsu
Niseishi
Sochin

Matsumuraha
(Shuri Shaolin)
Seisan
Bassai

Uechiha
(Fujian Tiger Gongfu)
Shimpa

Mabuniha
Jyuroku
Aoyagi (Seiryu)
Myojo

Note of Appreciation

I would like to extend my most sincere appreciation to the Konishi family in Tokyo, the Sakagami family in Yokohama, the Uechi family in Okinawa, and the Kuniba family in America for their permission to use many of the old photographs featured in this presentation. I would also like to thank Master Kinjo Hiroshi in Hiratsuka, for his personal recollections, old photos, and invaluable assistance. Finally, to my incredible wife, Yuriko, without whose support and assistance, much, if not all, of my research would simply not be possible.

Patrick McCarthy

2

Karate-do Gaisetsu: An Outline of Karate-do

BY MIYAGI CHOJUN
(MARCH 23, 1934)

Dedication

This modest interpretation is dedicated to all those enthusiasts seeking to get beyond the immediate results of physical training and transcend the barriers of ego-related distractions through the relentless pursuit of karate-doh; the way of karate-do.

Acknowledgments

I would like to extend my deepest appreciation to Konishi Takehiro Sensei of the Ryobukai, who granted me access to the original copy of Master Miyagi's handwritten manuscript—originally given to his father (Konishi Yasuhiro)—for this publication. I would also like to extend my most sincere gratitude to the Miyagi family in Okinawa for their permission to translate and reproduce this historic work in English. I would also like to thank senior Okinawan karate-do master and revered historian Kinjo Hiroshi, who unselfishly served as the special consultant in the interpretation of the old and very difficult writing style used by Miyagi Chojun, and for his postscript. I must also thank my good friend and colleague Hokama Tetsuhiro Sensei, author, master teacher of karate-do, and curator of Okinawa's only museum dedicated to the Ryukyuan fighting heritage. His endless support and friendship continue to be of immeasurable value to my ongoing research. Finally, I must acknowledge my lovely wife, Yuriko, without whose help and patience this translation would simply not have been possible.

I am deeply grateful to all,

Patrick McCarthy

Preface

As the son of Miyagi Chojun, I can hardly say what a great pleasure it is to see my father's 1934 outline of karate-do translated into English by Patrick McCarthy and the International Ryukyu Karate Research Society.

Having first met Mr. McCarthy in Okinawa, I was deeply impressed by his character and genuine concern to accurately chronicle the history of our native civil fighting heritage. I really hope that he is able to introduce my father's work and its valuable guidance to karate-do enthusiasts throughout the world.

Although much time has past since Sendai (Miyagi Chojun) was laid to rest, the radiance of his spirit lives on through the legacy he left behind. My father dedicated his entire life to the study of karate-do, and only through a deep resolve, immeasurable patience, and constant training did he finally master its deepest secrets.

Respected as a prominent authority of karate-do and the founder of a unique tradition, rarely is the term *goju-ryu* used without the mention of Miyagi Chojun. I am deeply grateful to all those who have supported my father's research in the past, and will continue to do so in the future.

My father deeply loved his family. He was a strict but kind man who, until the day he died, gave unselfishly of himself to his ten children, friends, and students. I sincerely hope that the material imparted in this document will bring you closer to understanding the

Way of karate-do, and knowing the man whom we all loved and respected so much.

Miyagi Ken
Naha, Okinawa

Foreword

Founding the Ryobukan in 1920, my father was already well established within the kendo and ju-jutsu community when he first got the idea of studying karate-do. Impressed with a demonstration of *kusankun kata* performed by an Okinawan named Aragaki Tsuneshige at my father's kendo bukatsu (kendo club) in Keio University, Sendai (Konishi Yasuhiro) began to study Toudi before it was introduced to the Japanese mainland.

Studying directly under Funakoshi Gichin, Motobu Choki, Mabuni Kenwa, and Miyagi Chojun during the Golden Era, my father realized that Ryukyu karate-do-jutsu, compared with judo and kendo, was not yet a complete form of budo. Thus it became his life's dream and vocation to elevate karate-do to the same level as Japanese budo.

A man of great vision who foresaw the future greatness of karate-do, Miyagi Chojun Sensei was a man who embraced a deep respect for the spirit of budo. A man of incredible conviction, Miyagi Sensei maintained that "the ultimate aim of karate-do was to build character, conquer human misery, and find spiritual freedom," a philosophy my father enthusiastically shared.

Sitting dormant within the sanctuary of my father's personal library, more than half a century has passed since Miyagi Sensei handwrote this very precious document. His message represents as much now as it did then, and provides a deep insight into a remarkable man.

I was delighted to find that Mr. Patrick McCarthy was so inspired to take on the task of translating Master Miyagi's original research. Mr. McCarthy is the director of the International Ryukyu Karate Research Society, and has a considerable background in both the classical and modern fighting traditions. Residing here in

....
41

Japan for many years, Mr. McCarthy is deeply committed to exploring both the evolution and spiritual value of budo. I am deeply impressed by his character and enthusiasm, and sincerely hope that his efforts are met with equal intensity.

Konishi (Takehiro) Yasuhiro
Ryobukai Hombu, Tokyo

Introduction

Those ancient Chinese principles of self-defense introduced to the Ryukyu Kingdom through the Ming Sapposhi[1] were, for the most part, pursued as a means of civil law enforcement by the pechin class called *keimochi*.[2] This was after King Sho Shin had brought feudalism to an end in 1507. Influenced through their contact with other foreign cultures and then radically affected by political oppression,[3] these principles of self-defense (not unlike any other feudal combative discipline) were vigorously cultivated beneath an iron-clad ritual of secrecy.[4] Gradually influenced by ancient customs, inflexible ideologies, and profound religious conviction, an indigenous eclectic movement unfolded that ultimately served as the platform upon which a new and modern tradition was established. Revolutionized by the competitive phenomenon and then proliferated through commercial exploitation, Okinawa's domestic self-defense legacy is, in many ways, a microcosm reflecting a diverse if not enigmatic evolution.

Profile of Konishi Yasuhiro

Konishi Sensei (1893–1983), the founder of the Shindo Jinen-ryu karate-do-jutsu tradition, became a principal authority of this discipline during the time that karate-do-jutsu was being introduced from Okinawa to the mainland. Having studied directly under Funakoshi Gichin (1868–1957), Motobu Choki (1871–1944), Miyagi Chojun (1888–1953), and Mabuni Kenwa (1889–1952), Konishi Sensei was also a prominent kendo teacher, an expert of ju-jutsu, and man of considerable wealth and position. Enjoying a close friendship with

Fujita Seiko (1899–1966)—the fourteenth head master of the Koga-ryu nin-jutsu lineage—he also gained the respect of Taira Shinken (1897–1970) and a myriad of other eminent budo authorities, including the reverent Ueshiba Morihei (1883–1969), the founder of aikido.

Konishi's pragmatic contributions have had a profound affect upon the growth and direction of modern karate-do. And together with his colleague and friend Ohtsuka Hironori (1892–1982)—founder of Wado-ryu ju-jutsu kempo—Konishi Yasuhiro remains one of the principal architects of modern karate-do.

Konishi Sensei maintained that the essence of karate-do is "neither to defeat nor be defeated." He concluded that self-mastery through karate-do, was only made possible through first transcending the boundaries of ego-related distractions. He often said: "Karate-do aims to build character, improve human behavior, and cultivate modesty; it does not, however, guarantee it."

Having written a number of books on karate-do himself, Master Konishi was truly dedicated to exploring the utmost value of the fighting traditions. In addition to the many contributions Konishi Sensei has made to the development of modern karate-do, his remarkable collection of written materials and unique photographs unquestionably disclose the great lengths to which this fascinating man went in order to deepen his understanding of the karate-do phenomenon.

Profile of Miyagi Chojun

Much has been written about Miyagi Chojun and even more is known about his training doctrines through the profound legacy this great teacher left behind. Yet in seeking to gain a deeper understanding of the man and his personal ideologies, we find little testimony written by Miyagi Sensei himself. Hence, it is in the unprecedented discovery of this document that we are now able to further disclose the convictions of Miyagi Chojun, one of modern karate-do's most eminent authorities.

Dated the twenty-third of March 1934, this handwritten composition, by a forty-six-year-old Miyagi, was titled *Karate-do Gaisetsu* (An Outline of Karate-do [Chinese-hand]). Composed just prior to his trip to Hawaii in April of 1934, Miyagi Sensei wrote this outline in an effort to introduce karate-do and provide a general explanation of its history, philosophy, and application.

It is no less interesting to observe that Miyagi Sensei, when writing the term *karate-do,* still employed the ideogram referring to "China" rather than using the modern *kanji* meaning "empty."

The Kara of Karate-do

A homonymic ideogram that can be either pronounced *Tou* or *kara,* Kinjo Hiroshi[5] assured us that up until around World War II the Uchinan (Okinawan) karate-do masters generally referred to karate-do as Toudi. First used by Kinjo's karate-do master Hanashiro Chomo (1869–1945) in his 1905 publication *Karate-do Kumite,* this unique ideogram characterized a plebeian art of self-defense using nothing more than one's empty hands to overcome an adversary.

Officially introduced to the Japanese mainland during the Taisho period (1912–1926), during an era of escalating militarism, modern karate-do was forged in the image of kendo and judo.[6] As with other traditional combative disciplines, karate-do came to reflect those spartan like cultural values of a homogeneous society.

As such, the new prefix *kara,* representing "empty" (i.e., empty hands), upon a deeper plane also embraced the ancient Buddhist doctrine surrounding spiritual emancipation and the world within, as did the suffix *do.* As such, the new ideograms proclaimed that Okinawa's plebeian discipline of karate-do-jutsu had transcended the physical boundaries of common brutality and had become a modern budo after embracing that which was Japanese.

Like other Japanese cultural disciplines, karate-do became another vehicle through which the Japanese principle of *wa*[7] was funneled. Hence, the innovative term *karate-do*[8] (the Way of karate) succeeded the term *Toudi-jutsu* (the art of Toudi) or karate-do-jutsu.

While the new term *karate-do,* using the two novel ideograms (*kara* and *do*), was not officially recognized in Okinawa until 1936,[9] it was ratified by the Dai Nippon Butoku-kai during December of 1933 when karate-do was finally recognized as a modern Japanese budo.

The Outline of Ryukyu Karate-do

The purpose of karate-do is often misunderstood by those who watch exhibitions of board-breaking and brick-breaking. This is not karate-do. In times of peace, karate-do should be pursued for its nonutilitarian purpose, such as the training of the mind. However, during times of lawlessness, one can use one's body to defeat an adversary.

It is quite difficult to put into words the purpose or true meaning of do. Like other forms of budo, its deepest meaning lies beyond written words; its essence transcends a simple written description. The following presentation represents one way through which to embrace karate-do.

The Origin of Karate-do

It is in Chinese kempo (quanfa) that we discover the source from which karate-do ascended. However, the actual evolution of Chinese kempo remains unclear because little historical documentation exists testifying to its development.

One theory suggests that kempo inherently evolved alongside mankind in the Middle East or Turkey from ancient times, and then found its way to India and China. Another theory describes the advent of kempo five thousand years ago in China, at the time of the Yellow Emperor.

Notwithstanding, we can only be sure that such a need to cultivate defensive capabilities resulted from the animosity that is inherent in human nature.

Reflecting this instinctive temperament, the most ancient methods of Chinese kempo were first based upon the fighting movements of birds and beasts. Hence, the names of the individual methods of fighting that reflected the source from which they ascended. By mere example: the tiger way, the lion way, the monkey way, the dog way, and the way of the crane.

Distinctive characteristics (based upon geographical, climatic, and social dissimilarity) caused Chinese kempo to divide into two separate factions. Known as the northern and the southern schools, they were further divided into internal and external systems.

Internal systems emphasized softness and pliability. Its defensive techniques were based upon evasive tactics, and were representative of wudang quanfa. External styles mainly emphasized technique based upon physical strength, and were best suited for brawny people. The hard or external schools trace their origins to the Shaolin temple located in Dengfeng county, Henan province, China.

Later, during the Tang (A.D. 618–907) and Song (A.D. 960–1279) dynasties, a number of martial arts heroes succeeded in bringing fame to the civil fighting traditions as they rose to prominence in China. Yet there remains little historical documentation testifying to the advent of Chinese kempo within the Ryukyu islands. Rather, there exists a myriad of suppositions.

Basically there are three major theories surrounding the advent of kempo within the Ryukyu's. The first is the thirty-six-family theory of Kuninda;[10] the second is the *Oshima Hikki*[11] phenomenon; and the third is that the Chinese fighting traditions were imported to the Ryukyu Kingdom sometime after the Keicho period.[12]

The Three Hypotheses

1. Kuninda

In 1372, some four years after the Mongols fell to the powerful forces of the Ming empire (1368–1644), Emperor Zhu Yuan Zhang sent a special delegation to Chuzan (the most powerful of Okinawa's three rival principalities) in an effort to negotiate a liaison between the two cultures.

By 1392—the twenty-fifth year of Emperor Zhu Yuan Zhang—Chuzan's King Satto (1350–1395) ratified the liaison with Ming China and approved the plans for a Chinese mission to be built in Naha's Kuninda area (present-day Kume village). This cultural phenomenon became known as the thirty-six-family theory. Including political, educational, and occupational specialists, it is believed that quanfa was first introduced through the security personnel attached to the mission.

2. *The Oshima Hikki*

In 1762, an Okinawan tribute ship, en route to Satsuma, drifted to Tosa (the old name for Kochi Prefecture in Shikoku, Japan). In charge of recording the testimony of passengers and crew, a Confucian scholar named Tobe Ryoen was petitioned by the *bakufu* (military government). On board was an important Ryukyuan official named Shiohira Pechin who provided a provocative account of the Chinese fighting traditions in the Ryukyu Kingdom.

In volume three of Tobe's chronicle, *Oshima Hikki,* there appears, during his dialogue with Shiohira Pechin, the name of a Kusankun who was an expert in kempo. Together with some of his disciples, Kusankun had come to the Ryukyu Kingdom (alternative sources would suggest that Kusankun came to Okinawa with the Qing Sapposhi named Guan Kui in 1756) where he referred to kempo as kumiai-jutsu. Although somewhat limited, the Oshima hypothesis appears to be the most reliable document concerning kempo in the Ryukyu Kingdom.

3. *The Satsuma Subjugation*

Following Keicho 14 (1609, the fourteenth year of Emperor Keicho) and after the Satsuma had disarmed the Ryukyu Kingdom and prohibited the possession of weapons, Toudi is believed to have been imported (or cultivated) intuitively. However, the theory that kempo[13] was introduced long before 1609 and then vigorously cultivated is a far more reliable supposition.

Beyond these three principal theories, other less popular hypotheses also exist. However, the plausibility of their authenticity is punctuated by inconsistent testimony. Notwithstanding, there can be no question that karate-do (in Okinawa) has been vigorously pursued and enhanced from long ago right up until the present time.

Karate-do in the Past

The origins within the Ryukyu islands surrounding the term *Toudi* also remains unclear. However, studies would indicate that it is a recent development. In the olden days, Toudi was simply refered to as *di* or *te* (a generic term describing those civil fighting traditions that were brought to the Ryukyu's from mainland China). In those days, Toudi—(that is, *te*)—unfolded into an iron-clad ritual of secrecy. Kata were only passed on to the very best students. Masters who were unsuccessful at cultivating students worthy[14] of learning their kata, were unable to pass on that unique tradition (meaning his kata) known only to him. Subsequently, that tradition was lost upon the master's death. Many traditions are thought to have vanished through this uncompromising ancient custom.

From the middle of the Meiji period (1868–1912), a time after Japan had transcended the restrictions of feudalism, the iron-clad ritual of secrecy that once enshrouded karate-do dissolved as public curiosity grew. As a result, many local experts prepared to meet the changing times as karate-do was largely being accepted.

Translator's Note

Although Miyagi Sensei does not actually spell it out, Kinjo Sensei maintained that the prefix *Tou* attached to the generic term *di* was a locally adopted term. By attaching the ideogram *Tou*—the old way that the Uchinanchu/Japanese (Okinawa people) described China— to the generic character *di* (meaning Chinese kempo), was a unique way of differentiating the indigenous Okinawan arts (Okinawa-te) from those of pure Chinese extraction. Kinjo Sensei stated that the term most likely unfolded during the Meiji period, when the various kinds of *ti* were being openly compared and discussed.

During that time, Toudi rose to prominence and became recognized as a way through which to improve one's health and conduct. Being introduced into Okinawa's school system only confirmed its acceptance and its beneficial value to Japanese society.

Karate-do in the School System

In April 1909 (Meiji 34), karate-do became a part of the physical educational curricula at Shuri Jinjo Sho Gakko (the old name for Okinawa's First Prefectural Middle School).

....

This was the first stone in the foundation of group teaching. Later, during the April[15] of 1905 (Meiji 38), three karate-do bukatsu (interschool karate-do clubs) were established in Okinawa—at the Kenritsu Dai Ichi Chu Gakko (Okinawa Prefectural First Middle School), at the Naha Shuritsu Shiyogyo Gakko (the Naha City Commercial School), and at the Okinawa Shihan Gakko (Okinawa's Teachers College). Following the establishment and popularity of these interschool clubs, others were soon formed.

By 1922 (Taisho 11), karate-do was being taught at Okinawa's Prefectural Police Academy. Then, in 1993 (Showa 8), karate-do, like jukendo (Way of the bayonet) became a part of the regular school curricula.

In March of Taisho 15 (1926), the Okinawa Karate-do Club was formally established. Then on November 21 of Showa 5 (1930), Okinawa's Prefectural Institute of Sports was established, which also had its own karate-do club. These represent the principal clubs of karate-do during that time. From Taisho 23 (1924), karate-do *bu* (clubs) surfaced in areas outside Okinawa.

Within the Toyko district the following clubs were formed:

Keio University Karate-do Club
Tokyo University Karate-do Club
The First High School Karate-do Club
Waseda University Karate-do Club
Nihon University Karate-do Research Society
Meiji University Karate-do Research Society
Takushoku University Karate-do Club
Shoin Girls School Karate-do Club
Nihon Medical University Karate-do Research Society

In May 1930 (Showa 5), a karate-do club was established at Kansai University in the Osaka district, and later that year, in December, another club was set up at their graduate school. I [Miyagi] also just learned that two other clubs were recently started at both the Osaka Medical University and Osaka Medical College.

Another significant point I wish to mention is a very proud day in the history of karate-do. On March 10 of Taisho 10 (1921), the

Crown Prince (who ascended as the Showa Emperor, Hirohito), en route to Europe, stopped over in Okinawa. It was on that visit that he observed a demonstration of karate-do at the Prefectural Teachers College. Four years later, during the May of Taisho 14 (1925), Prince ChichibuNomiya visited Okinawa on his way to England, and here he took pleasure in watching a demonstration of karate-do at the same Teachers College.

In September of Showa 5 (1930), Toudi was demonstrated alongside other forms of Japanese budo at the eminent Meiji Shrine in Tokyo. Two years later, during the May of Showa 7, karate-do was also presented at the Sainekan Budo festival (at the Imperial Palace in Tokyo). Similarly, a display was also provided for both Prince Kuninomiya and Fushinomiya, during the April of Showa 8 (1933), while they were anchored in Nakagusuku Bay (Okinawa) with the Imperial navy.

The Current State of Karate-do Instruction

Folklore contends that the teaching methods of long ago focused mainly upon self-defense, with little emphasis placed upon training the mind, or cultivating the precept *"karate-do ni sente nashi"* (there is no first attack in karate-do). I have observed the neglect of this diligent principle, although, with the passage of time, teaching policies have gradually improved to where that imbalance has, for the most part, been corrected. My conviction is that the fist and Zen are one of the same. Together, this balance cultivates intellect ahead of strength. The transmission of budo's essential precept must be fostered.

The teachers of karate-do within Okinawa include (in alphabetical order): Chibana Choshin, Gusukuma Shimpan, Hanashiro Chomo, Higa Seiko, Kamiya Jinsei, Kiyoda Juhatsu, Kyan Chotoku, Nakasone Kamato, Oshiro Chojo, Shinzato Jinang, Tokuda Anbum, Yabiku Moden, Yabu Kentsu, and myself.

Sensei outside of Okinawa Prefecture include (in alphabetical order): Funakoshi Gichin, Konishi Yasuhiro, Mabuni Kenwa, Miki Nisaburo, Motobu Choki, Mr. Sakai, and Sawayama Masaru.

About the Styles of Karate-do

Currently there are many theories about karate-do styles, yet none have been corroborated by historical investigation. Like fumbling in the dark, most theories are only vague suppositions.

The most accepted hypothesis describes the Shaolin and the Shorei styles. The former, it is said, best suits those whose structures are stout while the Shorei style best accommodates those with smaller frames, or who are thin like a willow and lack physical strength. However, after considering this from various perspectives it remains obvious that this evaluation is unquestionably erroneous.

The only detail we can be sure of is that during the eleventh year of Bunsei[16] (or the eighth year of China's Emperor Dao Guang), a Chinese system from Fuzhou unfolded and was studied deeply. From this did Goju-ryu karate-do kempo ascend. Even now this legitimacy still exists, and continues to be handed down.

The Special Merits of Karate-do

• A large space is not required.
• It can be practiced alone.
• Its practice does not require much time.
• Men and women, young and old, can practice karate-do; it depends entirely upon one's constitution.
• Proper kata can be selected, and practiced at one's discretion.
• One can practice with empty hands although the use of simple equipment may also be employed, and without much expense.
• Training in karate-do improves one's health. This fact is evident from the physical condition of aged enthusiasts.
• Physical and mental unity develops an indomitable spirit.

The Future of Karate-do

The era of secrecy in which karate-do-jutsu (the art of karate-do) unfolded has since concluded, and the time has come during this peaceful environment when karate-do (the Way of karate) can be pursued in public. In its infancy, the future of this Do (Way) is immeasurable. With this opportunity we must discard the narrow belief that karate-do is a secret art known only within the Ryukyu islands.

With karate-do open to the public, masters of budo need to continue to analyze and study karate-do to a great depth. In the future we expect to complete the development of safety equipment for competitive fighting. We are determined to have karate-do compete at the same level as other martial arts and in so doing karate-do will become a part of the Japanese martial arts spirit in general.

Karate is now enjoying a growth in popularity within both the Kanto and Kansai regions of Honshu and, indeed, throughout Japan. From Hokkaido to Taiwan, the study of karate-do is escalating while other martial arts throughout the nation are also exploring its value.

Furthermore, karate-do is flourishing overseas (surprisingly enough!). Devoted to the research and promotion of karate-do, there is a person who graduated from a university in Tokyo and has since journeyed to the West in order to encourage its growth.

In the United States (including Hawaii), the study of karate-do is also very popular. At the request of an influential businessman there, and in conjunction with his local newspaper publishing company, I have been petitioned to go, soon, to America. As I have already stated, karate-do is rapidly flourishing and will no longer be a budo exclusive to Japan, but will unfold as a martial art practiced worldwide.

The Methods of Teaching Karate-do

Our musculature development depends entirely upon the different ways in which we train. In order to better condition one's body for the practice of karate-do, *yobi-undo* (preliminary warm-up - exercises, now called *junbi-undo*) are performed prior to *kihon-kata* (fundamental exercises), *hojo-undo* (complimentary exercises), *kaishu-gata* (open-hand kata), and *kumite renshu* (sparring practice).

The following is a summary of these (exercises):

Yobi-undo (preparation exercises): Without expounding upon each specific exercise, preparation or warm-ups are performed so as to increase muscular flexibility while, at the same time, encourage strength and stamina. Warm-ups prepare one to better perform and learn the *kihon-kata* such as *sanchin, tensho,* and *naifanchi.* After completing *kihon-kata,* the *yobi-undo* are performed again in an effort to rejuvenate the muscle, followed by breathing exercises and relaxation.

Kihon-kata (fundamental exercises): *Sanchin, tensho,* and *naifanchi* are all *kihon-kata* that serve as practices for cultivating a strong physique while encouraging a budo spirit. Without expounding upon each specific exercise, students learn to regulate their breath while coordinating it with the use of their power in a correct posture.

Hojo-undo (complementary exercises): Without expounding upon each exercise, these drills are based upon techniques from various kata, and help one to better understand the *kaishu-gata* (open-hand formal exercises). Also performed with various kinds of apparatus, these unique exercises can serve to improve either a particular skill or overall proficiency.

Kaishu-gata (open-hand formal exercises): Without listing all the exercises, suffice to say there are twenty to thirty different kinds altogether. Many of them are named after their founders. Suitably interwoven, each kata combines both offensive and defensive techniques in various paradigms that one observes while practicing. Hence, it is through practicing these movements and understanding their purpose that one is brought closer to understanding the relationship between body and mind. In doing so, the principles of *toki* and *musubi*[17] can be cultivated.

Kumite renshu (sparring practice): In many ways *kumite renshu* encompasses the essence of *kobo no kata:* the application of those defensive and offensive activities within the kaishu-gata that are more representative of actual fighting. Through *kumite renshu* one may identify the practical meaning (or real purpose) of kata.

Summary

It is through combining the *kihon kata* (*sanchin, tensho,* and *naifanchi*) with both the *kaishu-gata* and *kumite renshu,* that a balance between body and mind is cultivated. Hence, it is through these offensive and defensive traditions that we seek to find truth and establish a budo spirit.

Miyagi Chojun
March 23, 1934

Postscript

As a general outline of karate-do, Miyagi Chojun's presentation makes a very deep impression! Written in an effort to help explain the karate-do phenomenon, Miyagi Chojun rationalizes its history, philosophy, and application. Ensuring us that the ultimate aim of karate-do, like other Japanese schools of budo, lies in transcending the physical barriers of common brutality, Miyagi Sensei underscores its spiritual magnitude.

Although Master Miyagi's outline is somewhat short in length, when compared to the other documents of that period it is, nonetheless, remarkably informative.

A sizable complaint (surrounding the introduction of karate-do-jutsu within the Japanese mainland during his generation) was the absence of an organized and unified teaching syllabi. This complaint, many feel, was never quite satisfactorarily resolved.

Considered gospel by all the other schools of Japanese budo, both the Okinawa-te and the Shuri-te disciplines had no organized or unified curricula, but rather an instructional format that varied from teacher to teacher. However, the fighting tradition established by Master Miyagi was based upon the southern Chinese gongfu style that his teacher, Higashionna Kanryo had brought from Fuzhou, and already had a basic teaching plan that was, and still is, unique.

In closing, Miyagi's 1934 "Outline of Karate-do" is particularly interesting, especially if one compares it with the 1936 version, which he drafted after returning from his trip to Hawaii. The subtle differences make for an interesting comparatives study. Any way you care to look at it, Miyagi Chojun's research is a valuable link within the historical chain of Okinawa's civil fighting heritage.

Kinjo Hiroshi
Hiratsuka

Okinawa, a turn-of-the-century photo with Higashionna Kanryo seated third from the left with Kiyoda Juhatsu directly behind him and Miyagi Chojun standing in the center.

May of 1934 in Hawaii, Miyagi Chojun poses with executives of the *Hawaii Pacific Times* newspaper company.

April 2, 1939, Naha Commercial School's karate-do club. Standing second from the right is Miyazato Eiichi, seated third from the left is Miyagi Chojun, next to him is the school vice principal Mr. Kiyoda, and beside him is Yamaguchi Masata.

November 16, 1925, Okinawa (masters and students). Seated left to right are Higa Seiko, Tahara Yazuzo, Mabuni Kenwa, Miyagi Chojun, Kiyoda Juhatsu, Shinzato Jinan, Manabashi Keiyo.

Summer of 1940, Miyagi Sensei poses in his yard with university karate-do club students visiting from the mainland.

July 13, 1942, outside the Okinawa Butokuden after a demonstration for a visiting dignitary. Seated third from the left is Nagamine Shoshin, third and fourth from the right are Miyagi Sensei and Shinzato Jinan.

December of 1942, Miyagi Sensei poses with members of the Naha Municipal Commercial High School Karate-do Club. Standing to the right of Miyagi Sensei holding sai is Iha Koshin.

Kakuzu Hill overlooking Makiminato in Okinawa, the final resting place of Miyagi Chojun; the Miyagi family tomb.

A close-up of the Miyagi family tombstone.

Right, Patrick McCarthy and Miyagi Ken in Naha's Kume village in front of the stone monument commemorating the lives of Higashionna Kanryo and Miyagi Chojun.

3

The 1936 Meeting of Okinawan Karate Masters

TRANSCRIBED BY PATRICK MCCARTHY
(OCTOBER 1994)

Introduction

Sponsored by the Ryukyu Shinposha (Ryukyu Newspaper Company), this historic gathering was held in Naha, Okinawa, on October 25, 1936 at the Showa Kaikan (meeting hall). In attendance were many of the island's most prominent karate-do authorities: Hanashiro Chomo, Kyan Chotoku, Motobu Choki, Chibana Choshin, Kiyoda Juhatsu, Miyagi Chojun, and Gusukuma Shimpan.

Special guests included Sato Koichi, the head of Educational Affairs; Shimabukuro Zenpatchi, the chief librarian for Okinawa Prefecture; Vice Commander Fukushima Kitsuma, regional military headquarters; Kita Ezio, a section chief from the prefectural police department; Goeku Chosho, a section chief from the Prefectural Department of Peace; Furukawa Gisaburo, director of the Prefectural Physical Education Board; Ando Shigeru, an author; Ryukyu Shinposha president Ota Chofu (1865–1938); Ryukyu Shinposha chief editor Matayoshi Yasukazu; Ryukyu Shinposha director Yamaguchi Zensoku; Mr. Tamaki, one of their journalists; Mr. Oroku Chotei, unidentified; and Nakasone Genwa, a karate-do writer/research historian.

Translated into English for the first time, the 1936 meeting reveals a wealth of original information through letting the reader evaluate the words and wisdom of those men responsible for shaping prewar modern karate-do. Furthermore, by studying this testimony we are able, for the first time, to understand why the name Toudi-jutsu was changed to karate-do, and why Okinawan's feared losing a piece of their cultural heritage. Evaluating the minutes of this historic meeting, first published in Toyama Kanken's 1963 book *karate-do Daiho Kan,* it is also possible to gain a deeper insight into the conditions leading up to the modernization of karate-do, and what, if any, prewar efforts were outlined for its unification and widespread promotion.

The principal force behind this gathering, Nakasone Genwa, was born in Okinawa and graduated from the Okinawa Teachers College in 1929. Having relocated to Tokyo he became involved with Japan's socialist movement, and served as the publisher of its newspaper. In 1934, he began to support and publish several books on karate-do. After the war, he continued a career in politics. In 1973, Nakasone authored *From Okinawa to Ryukyu;* however, to this day, Nakasone is probably best remembered for his brilliant 1938 publications, *Karate-do Taikan* and *Kobo Kempo Karate Numon,* the book he coauthored with Shito-ryu founder Mabuni Kenwa (1889–1942).

At the 1936 meeting, Nakasone Genwa (1886–1978) was fifty years old while Hanashiro Chomo (1869–1945), the former disciple of the legendary Bushi Matsumura (1809–1901) and a prominent senior master of Toudi-jutsu, was sixty-seven years old. Kyan Chotoku (1870–1945), a former disciple of Bushi Matsumura as well as being a prominent senior master of Toudi-jutsu, was sixty-six years old, and Motobu Chok (1871–1944), the most controversial figure of Toudi-jutsu during that era, was sixty-five years old.

Chibana Choshin (1885–1969), a former disciple of Itosu Anko (1832–1915) and the highly regarded master who first coined the term *Shorin-ryu* in place of Toudi-jutsu, was fifty-one years old; Kiyoda Juhatsu (1886–1967), the senior disciple of Higashionna Kanryo (1853–1917) and a prominent master of Toudi-jutsu who later founded the Toon-ryu tradition, was also fifty years old; Miyagi Chojun (1888–1953), the most well known disciple of Higashionna Kanryo and a respected master of Toudi-jutsu who later founded the Goju-ryu tradition, was forty-eight years old; Gusukuma Shimpan (1890–1954), a former disciple of both Higashionna Kanryo and Itosu Anko, and a respected master of Toudi-jutsu, was forty-six years old.

I would like to thank karate-do master Kinjo Hiroshi (1919–), a former disciple of Hanashiro Chomo, for providing me with an original copy of the minutes of this meeting, and for his assistance in helping to interpret the difficult-to-understand parts of this historically important work. Also, I would like to thank my wife, Yuriko, without whose help this translation would never have been possible.

Minutes of the Meeting

The meeting commenced at four o'clock in the evening.

MATAYOSHI YASUKAZU: Thank you for attending today. This meeting was organized by Mr. Nakasone Genwa. In addition to being with our company, Mr. Nakasone studies karate-do at the Shudokan in Tokyo, and is also a karate-do historian.

Recently, karate-do has become popular in Tokyo; however, in the midst of this popularity there seem to be some people who are practicing it the wrong way. We feel it is our responsibility to ensure that an orthodox tradition that embodies the painstaking efforts of Okinawa's authentic karate-do masters is the only discipline worthy of being handed down. Moreover, we are also concerned with the preservation and promotion of the research that both master and disciple have left us. I sincerely hope that everyone here today will candidly present their opinions.

We are fortunate to have with us today eminent karate-do authorities Hanashiro Chomo, Kyan Chotoku, Motobu Choki, and Miyagi Chojun. We would be truly delighted if you gentlemen could describe karate-do's true nature to us all today. With that in mind, Mr. Nakasone Genwa is now going to explain this meeting's format.

OTA CHOFU: All right, Mr. Nakasone, you have the floor.

NAKASONE GENWA: Thank you. As Ota and Matayoshi Sensei mentioned, I will speak first, even though I am just your humble *kohai* [junior]. Since my return from Tokyo two months ago I have interviewed many individuals regarding their opinions of karate-do and was disappointed to learn that Okinawa has no society uniting its various karate-do masters. However, we now have the means to establish such an organization through the Ryukyu Shinposha's support.

Karate-do should be vigorously fostered simply because it is an appropriate and effective budo through which to cultivate physical strength and indomitable spirit. I have been studying karate-do at the Shudokan[1] in Tokyo for many years [and] I am making every effort to disseminate the tradition. With that in mind, I would like to invite each of our distinguished masters here today to voice their opinions about encouraging karate-do throughout the entire nation.

In considering Matayoshi's suggestion, perhaps we should begin by addressing the issue surrounding the name karate-do. I would like to say that when karate-do[2] [written as "empty hand"] was first introduced in Tokyo, it was introduced as Toudi [written as "Chinese hand"]. At that time, karate-do was a novel tradition that took some time before gaining its popularity. Schools contended that Toudi was not a suitable term[3] and had, when writing the first ideogram of the term, used *hiragana*[4] rather than the Chinese ideogram.[5] Some dojo are being called Nihon Karate Kenkyu-kai [translated as Japan Hand Research Society]. However, that was during the transition period. Now, just about all dojo in the Tokyo area, including the two principal dojo, are using the new term *karate-do* [empty hand]. Most university clubs are also using the new term although there are still some university clubs that use Toudi [Chinese hand].

The reason for changing Toudi to karate-do is simply explained: It defines a tradition in which one uses the empty hands, or *karaken* [empty fist]. With that in mind, I would like to recommend that the current name karate-do [the way of the empty hand] becomes the standard in consideration of karate-do's future development as a Japanese budo. What do you think about my recommendation?

HANASHIRO CHOMO: In the old days, they did not say karate-do [empty hand], only Toudi [Chinese hand] or just *te* [hand]. That meant fighting with empty hands or fists.

OTA CHOFU: We called it Toudi, too.

SHIMABUKURO ZENPATCHI: Mr. Nakasone, karate-do has recently been called karate-do. Does this mean that the cultivation of one's spirit, like that of judo and kendo, will be emphasized? Is that why the "do"[6] was added?

NAKASONE GENWA: Yes. Its purpose seems to be the cultivation of the spirit.

OTA CHOFU: Mr. Miyagi, do you use the term *Toudi*?

MIYAGI CHOJUN: Yes, we use Toudi because it is in general use. However, it is a term used casually. Most people who come to my place wanting to learn usually just ask if I can teach them te. Judging by that, I would say that te seems to have been used before. I believe that the term *karate-do* is a good name because of what it represents. As Mr. Shimabukuro pointed out, judo evolved from ju-jutsu. In China, they used to call kempo, *beida* (white strike) a long time ago. Names change, like examples do, it depends upon the times. I prefer karate-do to just karate. However, I believe that the name must be unanimously decided upon by public opinion.

The Dai Nippon Butoku-kai branch has also discussed this issue among its committee members. Following that discussion, this issue has remained a pending concern. In China, the term *Toudido* is used. Soon a promotional organization (*shinkyo-kai*) will be established, and by that time we would like to see a purposeful name used.

OROKU CHOTEI: Mr. Miyagi, did you purposely go to China to study karate-do?

MIYAGI CHOJUN: Although I didn't begin training in China, I went there after realizing that it was the place I had to go for more advanced gongfu[7] studies.

OROKU CHOTEI: Is there a unique style of te here in Okinawa?

MIYAGI CHOJUN: Well, like judo, kendo,[8] and boxing, so, too, has the discipline of te been further cultivated and improved here in Okinawa.

KIYODA JUHATSU: I agree with Mr. Nakasone. Generally speaking, people of this prefecture are still familiar with the term *Toudi*. We should discuss this issue with the karate-do researchers here in Okinawa, and see what their analysis discloses. It's simply too early to decide here and now.

MIYAGI CHOJUN: I don't mean that we have to decide right here and now.

MATAYOSHI YASUKAZU: Could we hear some other opinions?

HANASHIRO CHOMO: In my old book *Karate Kumite,* published in August 1905, I used the term *karate-do* [empty hand].

FURUKAWA GISABURO: From our side, we'd like to promote it in the heart of the nation. We would like to see each prefecture establish an organization to promote karate-do, and a *shinkyo-kai* in order to establish karate-do within our junior high schools. In this way it will be possible to disseminate karate-do throughout all the prefectures. Then we can discuss ways to develop the discipline.

NAKASONE GENWA: I understand Mr. Kiyoda's opinion. We should consider the name and whom we should question. Should we decide by majority vote? Or should the people who enthusiastically practice karate-do decide? To help promote the art, the newspaper sponsors students who often travel around the island to lecture and give karate-do demonstrations. This will affect the growth and direction of karate-do throughout the entire nation. These youths recognize the term *Toudi* for its historical significance. However, they believe karate-do will develop under its own steam. I think that the volume of youngsters practicing karate-do, and their actions, will influence karate-do's future growth and direction. So Toudi should be changed to karate-do as soon as possible. We must not only consider its preservation but also its advancement.

KIYODA JUHATSU: Well, if everyone shares that opinion, I believe that the term *karate-do* will adequately serve the purpose.

GUSUKUMA SHIMPAN: Teaching in junior high school, I have found that students were not happy with the term *Toudi* and, subsequently,

I wrote kempo instead. However, I believe that supporting the term *karate-do* is proper because it refers to martial ways without weapons. Therefore, on this issue, I have no objections.

GOEKU CHOSHO: Connected with the Butoku-kai branch, I too, would like to say something. The Butoku-kai recognized karate-do as a martial way in 1933. At that time, Mr. Miyagi was still writing Toudi. So if the name is changed to karate-do, the Butoku-kai branch will rewrite and get approval. The branches will accept this change. At any rate, Butoku-kai *honbu* (headquarters) approval will be required.

OTA CHOFU: In 1905, Mr. Hanashiro was the first person to use the term *karate-do*. Anything that is popular in the heart of the nation [Tokyo] is customarily accepted all over the country. For example, Anshinbira [Anshin flat] in Naha has recently been changed to *habu-zaka* [habu-slope]. Also, the three-stringed instrument once called a shamisen is now called a *jabisen*. Names used in the heart of the nation are sure to become popular as in these examples. Okinawans might not be too happy about that, but if we are the only ones left using the term *Toudi,* when karate-do becomes a general martial way on the mainland, then I fear that people in the future will not come to know its Okinawan origins. Based on this point, I think that the term *karate-do* is appropriate.

NAKASONE GENWA: So far, we have heard from people who have lived in Okinawa for a long time. Can we hear the comments of Mr. Sato Koichi, the head of Educational Affairs, who recently came to Okinawa.

SATO KOICHI: I am not that familiar with karate-do, but Toudi doesn't seem to have much support among the experts. I think that karate-do should be used.

FURUKAWA GISABURO: For people from other prefectures, the term *karate-do* is appealing, and has a definite ring of martial arts to it. Moreover, it appears that Toudi has lost its appeal.

NAKASONE GENWA: May we also hear from Mr. Fukushima Kitsuma?

FUKUSHIMA KITSUMA: Well, karate-do seems to be an appropriate designation, especially if one is to consider the relationship between the name and the discipline: an art of self-defense using the empty hands.

NAKASONE GENWA: There's a story about a showman who was strong enough to pull a car. To draw attention to himself, he made a sign that read: Kojimaryu Toudi-jutsu.

OTA CHOFU: I don't think that anybody dislikes the term *kara;* however, there are those who resent the term *Tou* [China].

MIYAGI CHOJUN: When I visited Buwa,[9] the Chinese seemed to be familiar with the term *Toudi*.

FUKUSHIMA KITSUMA: Last year, the Physical Institution changed the name kyu-jutsu to kyudo. Like this example, a change from Toudi to karate-do should not be difficult.

KITA EZIO: Before I came to Okinawa I, too, believed that the pronunciation of kara (the alternative pronunciation for *tou*) meant empty.

OTA CHOFU: Originally, people in Okinawa used Toudi.

ANDO SHIGERU: I believe that China's Shorinji kenpo [Shaolin quanfa] is the original source of judo and Toudi. Therefore it is understandable that Toudi was used. However, I agree that the name should now be changed to karate-do [empty hand].

NAKASONE GENWA: It is incorrect to say that China's Shorinji kempo was the source of judo and karate-do. In Mr. Mikami Otokichi's novel, karate-do is described as Toudi-jutsu: A martial art that is partly foreign. This illustrates that karate-do is not generally understood that well.

SHIMABUKURO ZENPATCHI: They simply use te to describe karate-do in Okinawa, whereas Toudi is used to characterize self-defense methods from China.

NAKASONE GENWA: Well, it appears that we have discussed the name karate-do long enough now, so next I would like to ask you your opinions about the best ways in which to promote karate-do.

Unfortunately, karate-do in Okinawa is in a slump these days. Therefore, perhaps we should discuss ways to promote it from both the viewpoint of physical education and as a martial tradition.

FUKUSHIMA KITSUMA: There have been many karate-do sects established recently, but in my opinion we would be better off if they were all unified. Regardless of the differences between styles in Shuri and Naha, a unified Japanese karate-do kata curriculum should be established. Kendo used to have two hundred different styles, but they were unified into the present Japanese kendo kata. If karate-do can be unified, it, too, would be propagated throughout the nation. For example, let's say that we can:

1. Develop ten kinds of Japanese kata.
2. Use Japanese names for them.
3. Unify kata techniques and their contents to accommodate the principles of attack and applicable defenses.
4. Adopt a standard uniform.
5. Study the competitive element.
6. Plan tournaments for karate-do.

If we can accomplish these things, karate-do's form and substance will be unified.

MIYAGI CHOJUN: I quite agree with you. Concerning karate-do kata, I submitted my explanation to the Butoku-kai *honbu* when their branch first opened here. Concerning a standard uniform, we've often discussed this issue and would like to adopt one soon. Concerning technical terms, I'm confident that the time will come when they will be regulated. I have been insisting upon this issue and, in fact, I have already developed some new technical terms, and introduced them.

Concerning kata, perhaps it is better to develop and introduce a national kata, although the classical kata must remain. Suitable kata, with both the offensive and defensive, for students from elementary school to university level, should be developed. The *shinkyo-kai* should be responsible for developing and introducing these kata. There's the Physical Institution and the Butoku-kai branch here, along with our senior practitioners (*senpai*) and others who are interested in karate-do. We need to pool our resources and collectively research these issues.

If the experts and appropriate organizations conduct a thorough investigation, then the issues of terms, uniforms, and related problems may soon be concluded. However, classical kata must remain intact, otherwise they will be forgotten. New kata can always be developed.

NAKASONE GENWA: Sometimes varying technical terms can be a problem. It is difficult to present a lecture without standardized terms that can be universally understood. A gesture can only be understood if one has an audience. However, it is more difficult to make oneself understood in newspapers and other media. Therefore, the establishment of standardized technical terms is also necessary. Concerning competition, Teidai [the old name for Tokyo University, now called Toudai] and Kansai University are presently investigating the possibility of protective equipment that may gain more popularity in the future.

The old masters have preserved the classical kata because they understand the magnitude they represent. Karate masters vigorously study techniques; however, I believe that they remain too reserved when teaching their students. Because their teaching lacks enthusiasm [not sport-oriented], people generally lose interest. I think this is why karate-do is not as popular as it could be.

Therefore, I would like to recommend that a major organization, like a karate-do *shinkyo-kai,* be established where both experts and the general public can participate together for the art's advancement. For without the kind of organization and continued dialogue that we are sharing here today, the future efforts of individual master instructors will be inhibited. Therefore, I implore you to seriously consider establishing a karate-do *shinkyo-kai,* with the cooperation of people from various walks of life.

OTA CHOFU: We are definitely in favor of supporting that mandate. It is miraculous that karate-do has become so successful in Tokyo. We fully intend to support the movement, and I hope that communications between each group will be positive in an effort to establish the organization. How many karate-do groups are there now in Okinawa?

MIYAGI CHOJUN: Well, there is the Butoku-kai branch, the prefectural Physical Institute, the Shuri City Physical Institute . . .

OTA CHOFU: Mr. Chibana, how many students do you presently have training at your dojo?

CHIBANA CHOSHIN: Approximately forty.

MIYAGI CHOJUN: They say that karate-do has two separate sects: Shorin-ryu and Shorei-ryu. However, there is no clear evidence to support or deny this. If forced to distinguish the differences between these sects, then I would have to say that it is only the teaching methods that divide them.

Shorin-ryu's fundamental training [*kihon*] and open-hand techniques [*kaishu*] are not taught in any clearly defined way. However, the Shorei-ryu *kaishu* and *kihon* are taught according to a clearly established method. My teacher taught us according to the Shorei-ryu method.

OTA CHOFU: We have heard that (local) masters have not studied in China.

MIYAGI CHOJUN: I heard that Matsumura studied in China.

CHIBANA CHOSHIN: Our teacher taught *naifuanchin* for fundamental development.

OTA CHOFU: Mr. Motobu, with whom did you study?

MOTOBU CHOKI: Itosu, Sakuma, and Matsumora from Tomari . . .

OTA CHOFU: Mr. Motobu, didn't you make up your own style of karate-do?

MOTOBU CHOKI: (laughing) No, I did not.

NAKASONE GENWA: The establishment of a karate-do *shinkyo-kai* is a point of agreement by each master. As Mr. Furukawa described the necessity for a karate-do *shinkyo-kai,* we should agree upon each goal concerning this issue. The committee should start preparing for this project. (Each participant nods in agreement.)

OTA CHOFU: What organization is the Physical Institute?

FURUKAWA GISABURO: It is a semi-governmental corporation that the prefecture subsidizes. Every kind of budo and sport is included there.

OTA CHOFU: Do you mean that the Physical Institute will serve as the nucleus for the karate-do *shinkyo-kai?*

MIYAGI CHOJUN: Except for the Physical Institute there is also the Butoku-kai branch. Both organizations include karate-do departments. While the proposed *shinkyo-kai* will be associated with both the Butoku-kai and the Physical Institute, it will also stand alone as an independent organization of karate-do, like other budo organizations.

SATO KOICHI: Unified is better than independent.

OTA CHOFU: Will the karate-do *shinkyo-kai* be an organization representing one part of karate-do?

MIYAGI CHOJUN: Yes. In jukendo [bayonet discipline] they have a separate organization called the Yudansha-kai [Association of Dan Holders], which supports the judo and kendo departments of both the Physical Institute and the Butoku-kai branch. Similar to this, the *shinkyo-kai* will support the karate-do departments of both the Physical Institute and the Butoku-kai branch.

GOEKU CHOSHO: The requirements for dan grading in karate-do should also be unified. This will help to improve karate-do's growth and direction.

NAKASONE GENWA: It will be possible to do that as soon as the *shinkyo-kai* is established, and karate-do groups outside the prefecture have been united.

YAMAGUCHI ZENSOKU: As a sponsor, I would like to conclude the meeting with this. We have had a very productive meeting, the results of which will unquestionably affect karate-do's future growth

....

and direction. It is truly a great honor for the Okinawan people that our native karate-do has become so popular within the heart of the nation. Unfortunately, that popularity is not shared here in Okinawa.

Therefore, we must take steps to cope with the situation in an effort resolve the issue surrounding the name of karate-do, its technical terms, the unification of kata, and the establishment of the karate-do *shinkyo-kai*. Because children have a particular interest in this discipline, I believe that our purpose would be well served by introducing karate-do at the elementary school level.

Therefore, I will request the Educational Affairs Bureau to look into teaching karate-do in both elementary and junior high schools. If this proposal is adopted, I believe that our aspirations will be realized.

Meeting concluded.

4

The Dai Nippon Butoku-kai

BY PATRICK MCCARTHY

Virtues ahead of Vice. Values ahead of Vanity. Principles ahead of Personalities.

Introduction

Karate-do is the modern Japanese art of self-defense that cultivates health and fitness, character development, pacifism, and spiritual harmony through physical discipline, philosophical assimilation, and protracted but methodical introspection. Once vigorously cultivated by Okinawa's feudal aristocracy, karate-do emerged from native plebian grappling methods being synthesized with the Chinese gongfu traditions[1] that had been introduced to the tiny island kingdom over several generations. Today's numerous karate-do styles have surfaced due largely to each generation producing masters who found reason to reinterpret the universal self-defense principles and those moral precepts upon which they rest to better help the people they serve.

Compared to the fighting traditions of Japan's ancient samurai warrior, karate-do—an eclectic hybrid—must be to Okinawa's combative heritage what kendo and judo are to the classical schools of grappling and swordsmanship—ken-jutsu and ju-jutsu. Yet in seeking to understand the advent and obscure evolution of karate-do, we must turn our attention to those modern disciplines that have evolved from the classical combative traditions of the samurai warrior, their code of conduct, *bushido,* and the influence of the Dai Nippon Butoku-kai. By doing so the relationship between *bugei,*[2] *bushido,* the Dai Nippon Butoku-kai, and karate-do will become evident.

Bugei and *Bushido*

The samurai lived with a philosophy unique in the annals of mankind. Sometimes compared to the splendor of the cherry blossom, which falls from its bough at the moment of its greatest beauty, so, too, did the samurai warrior of ancient Japan live each day with the constant desire for beauty and perfection while preparing to meet his destiny.

Established during the rise of the warrior clans in tenth-century Japan, widespread military power struggles ultimately gave birth to the samurai class. The foundation upon which their combative disciplines ascended, and the Spartan code of conduct which, untainted by greed, became known as *bushido* (the way of the warrior).

Tightly bound by this warrior code, many regarded the samurai to be that culture's finest expression of *Yamato damashi* (Japanese spirit). *Bushido* required the samurai to pledge his very life to his master. For the samurai warrior, sacrificing one's life for one's master was a most glorious death. This philosophy, in which the samurai warrior lived to die gloriously, penetrated the lives of the common people. It was through this philosophy that *bugei* was perpetuated, further cultivated, and handed down to this very day.

Based upon *bugei,* various kinds of budo (modern martial ways) were established during Japan's post-Edo, pre–World War II era (1868–1937). Including kendo (Japanese fencing), judo (grappling), kyudo (Zen archery), naginatado (halberd fencing), jukendo (bayonet-mounted fencing), and karate-do, budo was not only a micro-cosm of the disciplined society from which it came, but it also served as a vehicle through which *bushido* was perpetuated, and so became an instrumental force in helping shape modern Japanese history.

With the abolition of the Tokugawa *bakufu* (the military gov-ernment that ruled Japan 1603–1868), the Meiji restoration deliv-ered Japan from feudalism into democracy. Hence, the class struc-ture and the wearing of swords—like the samurai warrior, their yearly stipend, and the *chongmage* (top-knot hairstyle)—faded into the annals of history, as did much of the other social phenomena representing feudalism's authoritarian forces.

However, unable to escape the powerful strain of masculinity under which Japan had evolved, and fearful of losing its homogene-ous identity in the wake of foreign influence, much of modern Japan's central tenets reflected its feudal-based ideologies. Perpet-uating old traditions while encouraging the development of many new social pastimes and cultural recreations, *bugei,* with its inflex-ible system of hierarchy, continued to be an instrumental force through which conformism continued to be funneled.

Based upon sport and recreation, the modern budo phenomena fostered a deep respect for those virtues, values, and principles re-vered in *bushido* that, in addition to other things, fostered the will-ingness to fight to the death or even to kill oneself, if necessary. Budo encouraged *shugyo* (austerity) and won widespread popularity in Japan during an age of escalating militarism.

Founded during the Meiji period (1868–1912), shortly after Japan ascended from feudalism, the Dai Nippon Butoku-kai was set up in the ancient capital of Kyoto in 1895. Built upon the ancient concept of fostering robust strength, indomitable spirit, and virtu-ous character, qualities encouraged by Japan's fiftieth emperor Kanmu (A.D. 781–805), the Butoku-kai perpetuated austerity and the moral principles upon which *bugei* first ascended, and revered the spirit of Kanmu as its patron.

Underscoring the magnitude of *wa* (an element of Japanese culture, perhaps better described as the readiness to sacrifice one's personal interests for the sake of harmonious communal unity),[3] the government authorized the Butoku-kai to research, preserve, and promote Japanese *bugei;* hold exhibitions and tournaments; collect weapons, equipment, and historical information on all classical combative traditions; and publish martial arts–related material. Thus did the Dai Nippon Butoku-kai became the example followed by everyone else.

On September 5, 1896, Emperor Meiji selected Komatsumiya Akihito, a member of the Imperial family, as the Butoku-kai's first sosai (general director). The following month, the association held its first Butoku-sai (martial arts festival) in a makeshift tent that featured kendo and judo exhibitions. The following year, the sosai and his cabinet of distinguished supporters vigorously lobbied and secured enough financial assistance from both the government and the emperor to establish an institute that could accommodate their growing membership, the Butokuden.

In 1899, the construction of the Butokuden (the Butoku-kai's official training hall) was completed and opened adjacent to the historically prominent Heian Shrine, located near Kyoto's Imperial Palace grounds. Serving as the Butoku-kai's *honbu* (headquarters), the Butokuden soon attracted Japan's most respected martial artists. In 1906, Fushinomiya, another member of the Imperial household, became the Butoku-kai's second sosai. Fushinomiya announced the organization's intention to establish a martial arts college. With a sizable grant from the Meiji emperor, the Butoku-kai embarked upon its plan. In June 1907 (Meiji 40), the Dai Nippon Butoku-kai became a Foundation.

With budo playing an important role in shaping the body, mind, and character of modern Japan, the Butoku-kai (in connection with the Education Ministry) was able, in 1911, to make both kendo and judo compulsory courses in all middle schools throughout the nation. Modern budo flourished in Japan's school system, signifying the value the government was placing upon budo training.

Embraced by an aggressive campaign of militarism, modern budo was often glamorized as the way in which "common men built uncommon bravery." Be that as it may, kendo and judo, during the post-Edo, pre–World War II interval, served well to produce strong, able bodies and dauntless fighting spirits for Japan's escalating war machine.

On September 18, 1911, the Butoku-kai opened its martial arts college, located next to the Butokuden. First called the Bujutsu Semmon Gakko (Martial Arts Specialty School), the name was later changed to the Budo Semmon Gakko (Martial Ways Specialty School), and nicknamed the Busen. One of Kano Jigoro's top disciples, the distinguished Isogai Hajime, served as the director of the Butoku-kai's judo department while the eminent Hokushin Ittoryu swordsman Naito Takaharu represented the kendo department.

In many ways, the Busen was regarded as Japan's West Point Academy. The mecca of Japan's fighting traditions, the Butokuden was where *budo juhapin* (the eighteen martial ways) were vigorously cultivated and highly revered. With both a two- and a four-year program and a host of brilliant instructors, the Busen disciplined its flock in kendo and judo while teaching military strategy, history, philosophy, and associated academic studies. This resulted in the forging of Japan's "new military mind," the modern samurai warrior. Graduates of this elite fraternity were revered as Japan's most skilled and highly educated experts of their day.

Under the auspices of the Butoku-kai, the martial arts encouraged *shushin, kokutai,*[5] and Nihonjinron (Japanese-ness), all of which are cultural elements that were deeply embraced by Japan's escalating war machine. During Japan's reactionary era of escalating militarism, it was the Butoku-kai that popularized the expression "Budo is the way common men build uncommon bravery," and branches were established in every prefecture to accommodate the growing popularity.

Titles and Ranks

Overseeing the country's entire martial arts community, the Butokukai conceived and issued the first distinguished titles for the modern *budoka* who were considered outstanding in their own particular disciplines. The first *shihan* (master teacher) titles were: *hanshi* (model expert or teacher by example) and *kyoshi,* originally known as *tasshi* (teaching expert); in 1934 a third title was introduced: *renshi* (well-trained or skilled expert). The Butoku-kai continues to issue these titles to this day.

The ranking system was, and still is within the Butoku-kai, the evaluation of an individual's progress toward the attainment of human perfection through the practice of the fighting traditions. This evaluation is not based solely upon physical prowess, but rather encompasses the individual's overall physical, moral, and spiritual development: budo's goal of cultivating our world within in an effort to enhance the world without. Hence, promotions were, and still are, awarded based upon this standard.

Some of the more recognizable experts of karate-do to have received the prestigious Butoku-kai titles have been: Mabuni Kenwa (Shito-ryu), Miyagi Chojun (Goju-ryu), Funakoshi Gichin (Shotokan), Funakoshi Giko (Shotokan), Konishi Yasuhiro (Shindo Jinen-ryu), Ohtsuka Hironori (Wado-ryu), Yamaguchi Gogen (Goju-kai), Nagamine Shoshin (Matsubayashi Shorin-ryu), Shinzato Jinan (Goju-ryu), Higa Seiko (Goju-ryu), Yagi Meitoku (Goju-ryu), Ueshima Sannosuke (Kushin-ryu), Tomoyori Ryusei (Kenyu-ryu), Kinjo Hiroshi (Koryu Uchinadi), and Sakagami Ryusho (Itosukai Shito-ryu).

Inaugurated by the Butoku-kai, the wearing of sashes and belts was conceived by the late founder of judo, Kano Jigoro. Kano was the brilliant innovator who foresaw the need to distinguish the difference between the advanced practitioner and the different levels of beginners; thus he developed the dan/kya system. The dan, or black belt, indicated an advanced proficiency level, and those who earned it became known as *yudansha* (dan recipients); while the kyu grade holders represented the varying levels of competency below the dan, and were known as *mudansha* (those not yet having received dan ranking).

Kano Sensei felt it important for all students to fully realize that one's training was in no way complete simply because one had achieved the dan degree. On the contrary, he emphasized that the attainment of the dan rank merely symbolized the real beginning of one's journey. By reaching black belt level, one had, in fact, completed only the necessary requirements to embark upon a relentless journey without distance that would ultimately result in self-mastery.

Having established the Kodokan dojo (Kano's training institute), Kano Sensei distributed a black sash to each and every *yudansha,* and this was worn around the standard dogi (practice uniform) of that era. Around 1907, the black sash was replaced with the *kuro-obi* (black belt), which became the standard used to this present day.

In an effort to regulate the competitive elements of budo, the Butoku-kai established a unique refereeing system that revolutionized their practice and also served to spread Japanese martial arts. Then, in December 1941, the Butoku-kai formed a committee to report upon the progress of the different budo groups. Konishi Yasuhiro (1893–1983, Shindo Jinen-ryu) and Ueshima Sannosuke (1895–1986, Kushin-ryu) were petitioned to report upon the progress of karate-do. The following year, owing to the war, the Butoku-kai was reorganized under the auspices of five ministries: welfare, education, war, navy, and national affairs.

In 1945, shortly after Japan unconditionally surrendered to the Allied Forces, the occupation forces prohibited all organizations considered to be the roots of militarism. With Prime Minister Tojo Hideki serving as head of the Butoku-kai during the war years, it came as no surprise that the Dai Nippon Butoku-kai, the Busen, and all its affiliates, were the first institutes ordered disbanded and closed after the war.

However, in January 1946, the Education Ministry was put in charge of the budo which were to serve only as a means of physical education within the school system. Later that year, former-Butoku-kai officials successfully made a strong effort to have the association reinstated; however, the judgment was short-lived, as senior Allied officials once again saw that it was terminated.

With the Butoku-kai dormant for the next seven years during the American occupation, various groups used its old *honbu,* the Butokuden. From 1945 to 1950, it served as the Allied Forces headquarters. Later, the Legal Affairs and Finance Ministries used it, then the Kyoto Police Department, and finally it became the site of the Tokyo Municipal Koto (thirteen-stringed *zither*) Association until it was declared a national treasure in 1970. Dilapidated, the old Butokuden was restored to its original splendor in 1987, although the surrounding buildings were torn down to make room for a new budo dojo.

Modern History

If there was ever any curiosity on Japan's mainland about Toudi-jutsu prior to the Dai Nippon Butoku-kai, it had to have surfaced from the attention gained when the Imperial army originally considered its value as an adjunct to physical training. With the draft invoked and Okinawa an official Japanese prefecture, the military vigorously campaigned there for local recruits. It was during the enlistment medical examinations in 1891 that two young Okinawan recruits (Yabu Kentsu [1866–1937] and Hanashiro Chomo [1869–1945]) were singled-out for their exemplary physical conditioning due to training in Toudi-jutsu.

Hence, the mere possibility that this little-known plebeian Okinawan fighting phenomenon might further enhance Japanese military effectiveness (as had kendo and judo) generated interest by way of a closer study of Ryukyu kempo Toudi-jutsu's potential value. However, the army ultimately abandoned its interest in Toudi-jutsu owing to impractical training methods, poor organization, and the great length of time it took to gain any proficiency (i.e., it was ineffective for boot-camp training as little benefit could be gained in six to eight weeks!). But that was not before an independent movement surfaced in an effort to modernize its practice, so Okinawa could make a significant cultural contribution to Japan's war machine.

Before the turn of the twentieth century, a small group of local Okinawan karate-do enthusiasts, headed by Itosu Anko,[6] organized a campaign to introduce this discipline into the island's school system as a form of physical exercise. In linking the past to the present, Itosu's crusade to modernize Toudi-jutsu resulted in fundamentally revising its purpose and practice.

Martial arts throughout the entire Japanese empire (from 1895 to 1945) fell directly under the jurisdiction of the Dai Nippon Butoku-kai, which, in turn, was accountable only to the Meiji emperor and his administration. As the sole agency in charge of budo in Japan, the Butoku-kai was supported largely by Meiji bureaucrats, the Ministry of Education, and the military. As such, any and all martial arts or related activities in the country were reported to, and invariably scrutinized by, the Butoku-kai.

Thoroughly impressed after having observed a demonstration while in Okinawa just after the turn of the century, Ogawa Shintaro reported his findings to the Mombusho (Ministry of Education), which resulted in Toudi-jutsu being recommended for schools within Okinawa Prefecture.[7]

By the end of the Meiji period, the practice of Toudi-jutsu had greatly improved and, with the emphasis placed upon the repetition of kata as the principle vehicle to teach large groups at one time, it served as a valuable adjunct to *taiso* (calisthenic group exercise) within the schools of Okinawa, thanks largely to Ogawa's endorsement, the efforts of Itosu Anko, and the new generation of teachers he had produced.

Although there is little testimony to support (or deny) allegations that it was developed in an effort to better prepare draftees for military service, Toudi-jutsu was introduced into Okinawa's school system under the pretense that young men with a healthy body and moral character were more productive to Japanese society and, hence, military service.

With the prefectural Mombusho authorizing Toudi-jutsu within Okinawa, it immediately became a concern of the Butoku-kai. Reports concerning the value of Toudi-jutsu since its improvement were not infrequent, and the enthusiasm of at least one young naval officer, one Rokuro Yashiro, made an enormous impression upon the Butoku-kai. Moreover, in 1912, with Japan's Imperial navy docked in Okinawa's Nakagusuku Bay (one week of naval maneuvers), officers and sailors eagerly sought out the worth of its defensive application.[8]

The praise Toudi-jutsu received from the Department of the Navy sparked widespread curiosity, which resulted in a petition being dispatched to Okinawa's Prefectural Mombusho, requesting that a delegation be sent to provide a demonstration before the Butoku-kai in Kyoto. Okinawa's Prefectural Board of Education subsequently asked one its teachers (Funakoshi Gichin, 1868–1957) to lead a small delegation. On May 5, 1917, Funakoshi and a small contingent of other local enthusiasts provided a demonstration together with an explanation of Toudi-jutsu for the Butoku-kai at the Kyoto Butokuden. This was the first official demonstration of Toudi-jutsu within the Japanese mainland.

Notwithstanding, it was upon this new foundation laid essentially by Master Itosu (Funakoshi's teacher) that a new generation of experts surfaced. It was during that generation of new experts that Okinawans such as Funakoshi Gichin, Motobu Choki (1871–1944), Uechi Kanbun (1877–1948), Miyagi Chojun (1888–1953), Toyama Kanken (1888–1966), Mabuni Kenwa (1889–1952), Gima Shinkan (1896–1989), and Chitose Tsuyoshi (1898–1984) found their way to mainland Japan, where they would introduce their own interpretations of Toudi-jutsu.

Cultural Forces

Ohtsuka Hironori (1892–1982, the founder of Wado-ryu) and Konishi Yasuhiro (the founder of Shindo Jinen-ryu) were two of the principal figures largely responsible for initiating the modernization movement that revolutionized Ryukyu kempo Toudi-jutsu after its introduction to mainland Japan. Konishi, a ju-jutsu expert and prominent kendo teacher, had studied Ryukyu kempo Toudi-jutsu before it was formally introduced to mainland Japan. He was the only man to have ever enjoyed the opportunity to learn under Funakoshi Gichin, Motobu Choki, Miyagi Chojun, and Mabuni Kenwa. It was Konishi who first told us that Toudi-jutsu, compared to judo and Kendo, was an incomplete discipline—at least by Japanese standards.

Konishi described modern karate-do as being forged in the exact image of kendo and judo.[9] By using the combative ethos of the ancient samurai warrior, fundamentally the various schools of ken-jutsu (swordsmanship) and ju-jutsu (grappling), an infrastructure was forged upon which modern budo was developed.

From the fundamental principles of ken-jutsu's most eminent schools, kendo was established, while the principal elements of ju-jutsu served as the basis upon which judo unfolded. Together, they provided the very guidelines by which Japanese karate-do was established: from judo came a lighter version of the standard dogi (practice uniform), the obi (belt), and the dan/kyu system; from kendo came the idea for establishing a teaching and grading standard for karate-do, along with protective equipment and the *ippon shobu*[10] concept for testing one's skills in competition.

Why?

In contrast to kendo and judo, the original Toudi-jutsu movement during the 1920s and early 1930s lacked a formal practice uniform and had no competitive format. Its teaching curricula varied from personality to personality and there was no organized standard for accurately evaluating the grades of proficiency, nor was there a competitive element to test the skills of the participants.

Compared to kendo and judo, by Japanese standards, the humble discipline of Ryukyu kempo Toudi-jutsu remained uncultivated and without suitable organization or oneness. In short, it was not Japanese. Ryukyu kempo Toudi-jutsu was subject to the criticism of rival and xenophobic opposition during that early and unsettled time of transition—when it was being introduced from Okinawa to the mainland during the 1920s and early 1930s. An old Japanese *kotowaza* (proverb) aptly describes how things and people can be . . . different (that is, not in balance with *wa*) and so are methodically thwarted by Japan's omnipotent cultural forces: *Deru kugi wah utareru*—a protruding nail ultimately gets hammered down.

The transition period was not short, nor was it without opposition. It included a justification phase and a time when animosities were ventilated, resulting in the winds of dissension carrying the seeds of reorganization. It was a time when foreign customs were openly discriminated against, anti-Chinese sentiment was rampant and so were methodically faded out, and more homogeneous convictions introduced.

Butoku-kai Influence

Representing centuries of illustrious cultural heritage, the Butoku-kai's ultratraditional *bugei* and budo cliques were deeply concerned as a result of the hostilities being openly vented between rival leaders.[11] This, together with the disorganized teaching curricula, lack of social decorum, and absence of formal practice apparel, testing standards, and competitive element, compelled the Butoku-kai to regard the situation as detrimental to Toudi-jutsu's growth and direction within the mainland, and set forth to resolve it.

The Criteria

The principal concern focused not only upon ensuring that teachers of Toudi-jutsu were fully qualified to teach, but also that the teachers actually understood what they were teaching. For Toudi-jutsu to be accepted within mainland Japan, the Butoku-kai called for the development and implementation of a unified teaching curricula, the adoption of a standard practice uniform, a consistent standard for accurately evaluating the grades of proficiency, the implementation of Kano Jigoro's dan/kyu[12] system, and the development of a safe competitive format through which participants could test their skills and spirit.

Although it was not the Butoku-kai that first proposed changing the name of Toudi-jutsu,[13] they were strongly in favor of using something other than a name that associated it with Japan's enemy: China. They were, however, responsible for the Toudi-jutsu movement abandoning the *jutsu* suffix, replacing it with the modern term *do* (as in judo and kendo) and played an integral role in having the ideogram *sora* (also pronounced *kara*) replace the character that connected Toudi to China. Just as one foot always equates to twelve inches, the plan was to establish a universal set of standards, as judo and kendo had done, so that karate-do's common principles could be clearly understood and easily impacted.

The Butoku-kai concluded that the improvements it called for would bring about a single coalition under their auspices, as had happened with judo and kendo. There is some uncorroborated testimony which maintains that Prince Nashimoto Moriwasa[14] empowered its founder, Miyagi Chojun, to set up a Karate Kyoju-kai (Karate Teacher Association) on behalf of the Butoku-kai in 1937 with Konishi and Sannosuke, in an effort to implement and oversee this transition. However, the continued development of karate-do was overshadowed by the widespread adversity of World War II, so much so that this universal set of standards failed to materialize.

Many believe that when the Butoku-kai (and other organizations considered the roots of militarism) were dissolved in 1945, after Japan unconditionally surrendered to the Allied Forces, the development of karate-do as a unified discipline was abandoned. However, like judo and kendo, karate-do did come to enjoy an untold popularity through the sport format born unto the school system.

In spite of karate-do's popularity, differences of opinion, personal animosities, protectionism, and fierce rivalry clearly illustrate that it is destined to maintain its individuality. While a myriad of eclectic interpretations continued to unfold, the traditional principles upon which karate-do rest have yet to be fully understood and brought together to form a single tradition; a phenomenon that, for better or worse, continues to this day.

Still a Vibrant Force

Thought to have vanished altogether, the Dai Nippon Butoku-kai was privately funded and reorganized in 1953 under the direction of the nucleus of its prewar membership. Higashifushimi, a member of the Showa emperor's immediate family, served as patron leader, and Ono Kumao, the prominent Hokki-ryu swordsman, sat at the helm of the once illustrious Butoku-kai. Located close to its original site, the Dai Nippon Butoku-kai *honbu* received permission to use the Shoren Temple in Kyoto's Higashi Yama-Ku, Awahta Guchi, where it remains to this day.

With the myriad of privately funded competitive martial arts organizations extant today, the ultratraditional Dai Nippon Butoku-kai remains overshadowed by the more highly publicized commercial associations. In spite of intense rivalry, this elite fraternity continues to foster essential precepts seemingly no longer fashionable during a generation dominated by materialism.

Although no longer exclusively in charge of budo in Japan, the Dai Nippon Butoku-kai still maintains that it is only through understanding the universal self-defense principles of this important cultural legacy, and those moral precepts upon which it rests, that the need for individual names and other ego-related distractions will ultimately vanish, leaving only karate-do, the combative heritage of Okinawa.

The Butoku-kai Insignia

The symbol for the Dai Nippon Butoku-kai is a beautiful and equally meaningful insignia. It takes its shape from the eight-point chrysanthemum, a flower first introduced to Japan in A.D. 650, from China. The nectar extracted from this ancient flower was, at that time, made into a wine that was thought to have ensured longevity. The flower became associated with the emperor, and ultimately became the national flower of Japan, which is still remembered every year on September 9.

The insignia is made up of gold characters upon a royal purple background, and is symbolic: the color gold represents the idea of richness. The Butoku-kai believes that the generations of learning transmitted through budo is an invaluable asset to its supporters. The royal purple, the official color of the emperor, represents the virtuous ideology that serves to govern the behavior of its supporters. The eight-point circumference of the flower represents the conceivable gates of attack and defense, a principle that unites all combative disciplines.

The Chinese characters *butoku* represent the martial virtues of the feudal samurai: respect, compassion, gratitude, loyalty, honor, and integrity. The rays emanating from its center represent the various *koryu* (feudal combative discipline) that served as the platform upon which budo was established. And lastly, there is the archer's bow and two arrows—these represent Japan's first line of military defense during its feudal beginnings.

References

Dai Nippon Butoku-kai Riyaku Reiki (a short history of the Dai Nippon Butoku-kai) published by the Butoku-kai, Kyoto, 1987.
Dai Nippon Butoku-kai Kaiho (Butokukai quarterly newsletters, from 1987).
The cooperation of Konishi Takehiro, Sugino Yoshio, Matsushita Kyocho, and the Kyoto Butoku-kai Honbu.

5

....

Karate-do: Development, Essence, and Aims

BY PATRICK MCCARTHY

Introduction

Budo, of which karate-do is a part, is a vehicle through which people can come to know the ritualistic, ethical, and spiritualistic values of old Japanese culture. If one wishes to truly understand karate-do it becomes necessary to study its underlying principles, rather than just practicing the physical techniques. Learning techniques indiscriminately without really understanding these principles is one of the primary reasons karate-do has become such an obscure tradition.

Karate-do is, in many ways, a microcosm of the disciplined and idealistic society from which it comes. So, too, are the Japanese a disciplined and idealistic people, and budo (as practiced in their country) is also idealistic and disciplined. Built upon ancient customs, inflexible ideologies, and profound spiritual conviction, modern Japanese society is, for the most part, still very much bound by cultural rituals. Rituals, for the Japanese, serve to teach important lessons about life—the obstacles one may encounter, how others have overcome them, and what to ultimately expect. Ritual is the platform upon which karate-do is taught, and it is through ritual that one's attention is ultimately turned inward to where a lifelong journey for spiritual harmony is pursued.

I have prepared this discourse in an effort to describe the men, myths, and rituals of karate-do by examining its historical framework, philosophical and spiritual precepts, therapeutic value, orthodox kata, and the application principles to which they apply. I sincerely hope that my presentation might serve to answer some of your questions about the Japanese art of karate-do.

Frequently provided with the opportunity to lecture upon karate-do, I feel that the widespread interest in the Japanese combative traditions provide its followers with more than just a promise of self-defense and fitness. However, one's potential for discovering the essence of budo, in general, depends largely upon the wisdom of the teacher responsible for transmitting the discipline.

In his 1991 book *The Forge of the Spirit: Structure, Motion and Meaning in the Japanese Martial Arts,* John J. Donohue suggests the following:

> The allure of the martial disciplines stems from the fact that they constitute ritual performances that symbolically deal with the fundamental questions of human existence: mortality; the quest for control, mystery, and power; and the search for identity. Our sense of mortality is heightened by increased fears of street violence and dissatisfaction with society. The symbolic re-creation of danger through the practice of the fighting traditions can provide us with the illusion of control over such events. The mysterious component of Asian fighting arts is often associated with the development of paranormal skills nestled in a matrix of "occult knowledge" that transcends everyday life experiences. The ongoing practice and rehearsal of techniques coupled with the review of underlying philosophical precepts serves to foster a sense of individual and personal accomplishment. Participation in practices with large groups of people sharing common beliefs provides an individual with a greater sense of identity, as well as a sense of place and purpose in life. One seeks to integrate and

"ground" oneself on these different levels: physical, psychological, social, and metaphysical.[1]

In recent years there has been growing interest in karate-do as an art rather than as a competitive activity or self-defense. However, unlike the immortal names—Tsukahara Bokuden, Miyamoto Musashi, Yagyu Munenori, or even the distinguished Zen prelate Takuan Soho (men who have magnified the gravity of martial arts in Japanese history)—the unsung heroes of karate-do have achieved a spiritual impact of less vibrant proportions. When we think of karate-do in general, the immediate image that comes to mind is a highly competitive sport, effective means of self-defense, and perhaps even an interesting alternative to conventional methods of physical fitness. However, I doubt seriously whether many people really think of karate-do in the same way they might think about Japanese swordsmanship, Zen archery, or even aikido.

For example, if karate-do was compared to Japanese swordsmanship, Zen archery, or aikido, what differences and what similarities would we discover? Of course, the obvious differences are quite apparent, but what about the principles of subjugation? How about the philosophical values, moral precepts, and spiritual teachings upon which they rest? Considering the possibility of such similarities, I wonder, then, when is it appropiate to acknowledge their existence? Whose responsibility is it to transmit them? Why are they not at the forefront of karate-do? Are they worth learning in the first place? Is it not enough that I have achieved a healthy body, a confident personality, and the ability to defend myself, if and when the need ever arises?

A practice popularized by Japan's samurai warrior, it is said that if and when austerity is balanced by philosophical assimilation and protracted by methodical introspection, one's attention is drawn deeply inward. There, captured by the essence of self-analysis, one is able to transcend ego-related distractions, and achieve an understanding that goes beyond physical training, punching and kicking, winning or losing.

Without much information available on karate-do, as an art, in the Western world, it is a great privilege for me to speak to you on this little known subject. In drawing your attention to the nonutilitarian values of karate-do, I would like to conclude my lecture by addressing the *do* of karate-do and determine whether or not it is truly a necessary consideration in an environment outside the pensive society and monastic sanctuary from whence it originally came.

The IRKRS

Before I begin this presentation, I would like to briefly explain what the International Ryukyu Karate Research Society is. Born out of pure necessity, the Society surfaced as an outgrowth of my ongoing research in Japan. Since that time, it has remained a small, self-funded, impartial group of researchers/writers/practicing budo enthusiasts dedicated, but not limited, to the analysis, preservation, and promotion of orthodox Okinawan karate-do and kobudo, herein referred to as koryu uchinadi.

Using koryu uchinadi as the central vehicle for self-improvement, our principal focus is to preserve and promote both the utilitarian and nonutilitarian (physical and metaphysical) elements of this art form. When deeply embraced, koryu uchinadi can enhance the value of each and every day of one's life, and it is to that end that our analysis continues.

With no competitive ambitions, we do not consider ourselves a threat to political organizations. Hence, the society has remained comfortably neutral in its sole purpose of gaining only the deepest knowledge of karate-do history and those principles upon which it rests. Both students and teachers of various karate-do organizations frequently explore the value of our latest discoveries in an effort to enhance the understanding of their own styles. In doing so, we believe that everyone benefits, and the ever-growing sphere of knowledge that brings us all closer together in goodwill and friendship provides not only a clearer understanding of this ancient tradition but of life in general.

Karate-do evolved from man's efforts to know the true meaning of victory and defeat through the use of his empty hands in combat. Practicing the way of karate-do, it becomes possible to achieve a state of understanding that transcends winning or losing. Karate-do teaches one to live in harmony with nature rather than frivolously trying to dominate or destroy it or, as my teacher Kinjo Hiroshi likes to say, "Karate teaches one to cooperate with the infinite, rather than continue to resist the inevitable." In an effort to attain its goal of perfection, karate-do, the art, fosters physical fitness, character development, and pacifism through balancing physical conditioning and philosophical assimilation with nutritional intelligence and protracted introspection. Such training results in a richer life through a deeper understanding of the self, and an appreciation of humanity.

While supporting its utilitarian values, the Society strongly believes that karate-do, like other forms of Japanese budo, can also serve as an effective vehicle through which to discover and explore one's "world within." The ultimate result of such a pursuit can only serve to enrich one's "outer world." It is said that an army of ten thousand can be defeated in battle but not an idea whose time has come. The Society represents a study of those infinite principles upon which all karate rests, and advocates understanding them in an effort to recognize the universality of all its interpretations.

Since my youth, I have vigorously followed many of the greatest martial arts masters of our time, and have done my utmost to assimilate, but not be bound by, the rituals, principles, and applications of their profound traditions. In many ways, this lecture brings together the essence of those discoveries that have made a significant impact upon shaping the way I embrace karate-do, in the way I assess its evolution and my personal philosophy with regard to its future direction.

The Motto of the International Budo University (Japan)

Through the pursuit and spirit of *budo,* youth forge a steadfast and principled philosophy of life, establish a peace-oriented view of the world in which they dwell, cultivate physical strength, learn the values of courtesy and patience, and pave the way for international friendship through sportsmanship.

—Dr. Matsumae Shigeyoshi
(1901–1991, founder of the Budo University)

Background

What is karate-do? From where did it come? Who created it and why? How did it evolve? Which forces effected its growth and direction? Of what value is karate-do within a modern society? More specifically, how can karate-do enhance the value of one's everyday life?

Karate-do is often described as an exciting and challenging sport, a fascinating cultural recreation, a practical form of self-defense, a rewarding social activity, a way of getting into shape and keeping fit, and sometimes even a way of combating the stress-related obstacles that so often impede an otherwise productive life.

Actually, karate-do is all of these things . . . and more. Based on ancient self-defense principles, karate-do is a modern Japanese art of self-defense that fosters character development and pacifism through physical discipline, philosophical assimilation, nutritional intelligence, and protracted but methodical introspection. In the Western world, everyone knows what a healthy body and clean life-style can do for an individual, yet the nonutilitarian elements of karate-do—that is, its metaphysical elements—have yet to be fully measured or completely understood here in the West.

In short, karate-do, the way of karate, teaches one how to live in harmony with nature rather than trying to dominate or destroy it. And while sport karate-do (the variety of karate-do with which most of us in the West have become familiar) is less than fifty years old, the original foundation upon which it rests dates back deeply into the annals of early Chinese history.

Modern Japanese karate-do evolved from an ancient Chinese self-defense discipline called quanfa,[2] which was once cultivated in feudal Okinawa during their protracted liaison with the Middle Kingdom (China). Once a popular practice among Okinawa's *kemo-chi*[3] in lieu of the prohibition on weapons, the principles of quanfa were ultimately cultivated by the pechin[4] as an adjunct to domestic law enforcement.

Interpreting the Japanese word *karate-do,* we discover a term comprised of three separate Chinese ideograms: *kara* (empty), *te* (hand[s]), and *do* (way or road). In the context of martial arts, this term literally means "empty hand way," which, on the surface, describes a unique method of defending oneself without the use of weapons. However, another meaning for these Chinese ideograms, one that is not readily apparent, encompasses a profound philosophy often referred to as "a way of life."

Reevaluating the alternate interpretation of these three Chinese ideograms, we discover that the term meaning "empty," pronounced *kara,* also means "void," which characterizes ancient spiritual doctrines popularized in Daoism and Buddhism. The term for "hand(s)," pronounced *te,* was the old way Okinawan's described the Chinese gongfu that had been cultivated on their island before the turn of this century (another term that also was used was Toudi-jutsu, *Tou* referring to "China" reveals the actual origins of *te,* while the suffix *jutsu* is a common way of describing a technique or teaching method or school). Finally, the term meaning "way" or "road," pronounced *do,* also identifies the inward path upon which its followers travel, while pursuing its spiritual principles.

A popular misconception maintains that karate-do, as we know it within the Western world, dates back far into the annals of Japan's feudal history and is, in some way, associated with the samurai warrior. Actually, nothing could be farther from the truth. Yet, like kendo and judo (two modern fighting traditions based upon combative disciplines once vigorously cultivated by the samurai of ancient Japan), ken-jutsu (swordsmanship), and ju-jutsu (grappling), karate-do is based on much older self-defense precepts, precepts originally brought from China. Culminating in years of combined effort, karate-do became officially recognized as a modern Japanese budo (martial ways) in December 1933, with its acceptance by the Dai Nippon Butoku-kai, the national governing body of budo in Japan.

In March 1934, just a month before he set off for Hawaii, Miyagi Chojun (1888–1953), the founder of Goju-ryu, when talking about the origins of karate-do, wrote a provocative message: "Regardless of where or when the civil fighting traditions first unfolded, we can only assume that they must have ascended alongside mankind from ancient times, due to the animosity inherent in human nature."

In seeking to better understand karate-do, it becomes necessary to explore its origins. However, the problem that arises when studying karate-do's evolution is that we discover a history shrouded in both myth and mysticism. To further complicate matters, records (if in fact any ever existed in the first place) appear to have been destroyed during the bombing devastation of Okinawa in 1945—a holocaust that, in addition to destroying the island's central populated areas, also claimed some 200,000 lives. That which remains has been handed down by oral tradition: word of mouth, folklore, and a few scraps of written testimony. Perhaps by analyzing that which we do know, and working backward in a logical order, cross-referencing and comparing known facts with corresponding information whenever possible, it may be possible to discover that which is currently outside our knowledge.

A Capsule History of Karate-do

Unsupported suppositions would have us believe that Okinawa's civil fighting legacy ascended from the subjugated huts of the pre-Meiji peasant class. Tyrannized by their overlords, it is said, the peasants, in an effort to break free from the chains of oppression,[5] had allegedly conceived an omnipotent fighting art.

Despite their uncultivated skills, it has always been hypothesized that the incomparable combat principles had somehow been applied to the implements used in their daily life. Furthermore, under the cover of total darkness, because they feared reprisal if caught, the peasants not only established this cultural phenomenon but also handed it down for generations, unbeknownst to the local authorities.

Supported by mere threads of historically inaccurate testimony, one discovers that the pre-Meiji peasant class supposition can no longer support the weight of serious consideration. Nonetheless, the peasant has been erroneously credited with the development of both Okinawa's weapons and empty-handed combative traditions while a more devoted study of the Ryukyu Kingdom reveals findings that suggest a more plausible explanation.

By nature, Okinawa has evolved as an island community of farmers and fishermen, but because of its suitable geographic location (between Japan, China, and the rest of Asia) it has ultimately became a bustling mid-point for trading and shipping. Yet, threatening this ascending prosperity, internal power struggles kept much of Okinawa's early history contained in feudal conflict. In an effort to bring an end to civil war, the newly centralized government of King Shoshin in 1507 methodically prohibited the use and stockpiling of weapons.

A feudal history of political and military subjugation generated a catalytic matrix in which Okinawa's disarmed aristocrats contrived an ingenious alternative for protecting themselves, their families, and their domain. By applying combative principles to a myriad of domestic objects, an eclectic method of self-defense was thus contrived. Serving as an effective adjunct to domestic law enforcement, embryonic fighting skills continued to be cultivated over many generations. Indiscriminately enhanced through the introduction of both Chinese and Japanese martial arts, these techniques were collected, studied, and reinterpreted. Combined with the quanfa disciplines, this process ultimately resulted in codifying many of the most popular practices from which came the establishment of kobudo (literally, "ancient martial ways") and Toudi-jutsu, now referred to as koryu uchinadi. Becoming a popular practice, especially among law enforcement officials of Okinawa's pechin class, much of this legacy has been preserved and passed on to this day.

Kata

Presently, there are various karate-do styles as each generation produces innovators (masters) who, in an effort to keep the tradition a living experience for the people it serves, reinterpret the universal self-defense principles upon which karate-do rests. The ritualized method in which the secrets of these traditions have been customarily transmitted is called kata, karate-do's paragon of mystery.

In recent times, karate-do masters have characterized kata as the very soul of karate-do. It has been said that kata is more than just the physical requirements from one grade to the next, or even a popular competitive event that requires its athletes to begin and conclude their performance on the same spot. However, if kata is more than just an adjunct to training (a somewhat tedious and monotonous practice, as teachers maintain) then where can we find a satisfactory analysis of this obscure phenomenon?

Seemingly a riddle wrapped in a mystery inside an enigma,[6] kata is now more than ever the subject of intense curiosity as modern karate-do prepares to enter the twenty-first century Because we know that the orthodox Okinawan karate-do kata were originally brought from China or based upon those Chinese defensive paradigms, it would then make some sense to examine the history of the *hsing* (kata) of Chinese quanfa in an effort to better understand its history.

In so doing, the reason for kata's development, why it evolved into an iron-clad ritual of secrecy, and how it was finally transformed into a Japanese cultural recreation might then all be revealed.

The *Hsing* of Chinese Quanfa

The *hsing* (kata in Japanese) of quanfa is the ritualized method through which the secrets of self-defense have been customarily transmitted for generations in China. Addressing a myriad of conceivable attack scenarios, each *hsing,* a unique tradition of their own, consists of preordained self-defense responses to the habitual acts of physical violence that plagued the period in which they were brilliantly contrived.

In the annals of quanfa history, these defensive applications were originally contrived to restrain, incapacitate, maim, or even kill an adversary if absolutely necessary.

Prehistoric Hypothesis

Like wild animals, one of man's most instinctive mechanisms is survival. And like an animal, if man's survival is threatened and escape impossible, his basic instinct is to fight. However, unlike the wild beasts he must have confronted, prehistoric man was not endowed with natural defensive weapons like strength, speed, claws, or sharp teeth, and had to instead rely upon his ingenuity and adaptability. Therefore, early man must have first instinctively tried to use his limbs as defense tools before ultimately turning his attention to using nearby objects before he discovered how to contrive and use proper weapons to support his existence. No doubt these principles served as the earliest means of attack and defense for prehistoric man.

It would seem likely that when prehistoric tribesmen gathered around to feast and recount the events of the battle or hunt, a seed was planted from which a primitive self-defense ritual was born. Fighting techniques employed during the hunt or in battle, no doubt at the cost of human life, formed the basis upon which more effective attack and defense discoveries were later extrapolated and then further cultivated. Reenacted within the sanctuary of the tribe, young boys (future warriors) being brought up in an environment of discipline, vigorously imitated the fighting techniques demonstrated by their elders in an effort to learn the "way(s) of the warrior." Hence, it seems perfectly plausible that in these primitive circumstances, the ritual for teaching self-defense skills was first contrived, cultivated, and perpetuated.

In a 1985 personal conversation, Sid Campbell, the American karate-do pioneer, author, and martial arts historian, supported this hypothesis by suggesting that "since the earliest times, from before written records, man best conveyed his ideas by way of verbal gesture and physical emulations. By doing so, he not only established a means through which to preserve and pass on his knowledge, he also provided a way through which to create a more refined methodology."

From tribal chieftain to village warrior, from father to son, from mother to daughter, or from master to disciple, combative paradigms have, from before recorded history, continued to serve as the principal vehicle through which the secrets of self-defense have been safeguarded, perfected, and transmitted.

Affected by both climate and geography,[7] self-defense methods became entwined with that society's local customs, language, rituals, etiquette, dress, and metaphysical ideologies. Then, as man began to expand the boundaries of his domain, his native self-defense methods were ultimately affected by foreign influence, which resulted in the evolution of a myriad of eclectic traditions.

Self-defense methodologies, regardless of where they evolved, were cloaked in rituals of secrecy so that their tactics would remain concealed.

The Effect of Spirituality on Self-Defense

The tenets of spirituality were also born during ancient times and vigorously cultivated by shamans and medicine men to exercise power over their people. By the time sages began to lead the small communities, more emphasis was placed on spiritualism in an effort to bring order to the otherwise primitive tribes of man; they came to understand that it was far better to live in harmony with nature than try to dominate it.

The most successful spiritual factions within man's ancient communities effectively cultivated remarkable doctrines that provided illuminating paths upon which followers, through methodical self-diagnosis, discovered the source of human suffering. In an effort to protect their spiritual beliefs and maintain a robust health, spiritual recluses cultivated herbalism, physical exercise, and systems of self-defense to protect such convictions. The legendary place that cradled this unique historical synthesis is reputed to be China's Shaolin Monastery.

It would be ludicrous to even consider that self-defense methods did not exist in ancient China prior to the advent of the Shaolin order. However, the advent and subsequent development of a codified self-defense system (i.e., quanfa) together with spiritual characteristics and a moral philosophy with which to govern the behavior of those who mastered its secrets, remains purely a cultural phenomenon cradled within the confines of China's austere monastic sanctuaries.

Being synthesized within such an inflexible environment, especially during China's Daoist-oriented period, it is easy to understand how society profoundly affected the evolution of quanfa. Introduced from India and assimilated into ancient Chinese Confucian society, embryonic, spiritual practices and esoteric principles formed the foundation on which quanfa developed. This synthesis included ritualistic *vajramukti* health exercises for strengthening bone, tendon, and muscle; defensive techniques from *ksatreya* warrior traditions; meditative breathing methods and yoga *asana* postures; acupuncture, massage, and herbal medicine; and Buddhist spiritual doctrines, all introduced by Indian missionary monks.

Yet when introduced outside its monastic sanctuary, the moral, philosophical, and spiritual elements of quanfa became detached, reduced to a ritual of lip service. This resulted primarily because its defensive techniques were often sought after by secular disciples, many of whom placed little or no importance on its moral or spiritual purposes. In modern times, its moral and spiritual elements have all but disappeared.

Grappling

In frivolously trying to establish a genealogical pedigree between the ancient self-defense traditions, it is interesting to consider the development of grappling. In Greece, wrestling traces its history all the way back to around 704 B.C., when it was first introduced as a sport at the eighteenth Olympiad. In addition to basic grappling skills, wrestling, during that ancient period, also employed striking, strangulation techniques, head-butting, and kicking. Although its source of origin remains unknown (it is believed to have been introduced from Mesopotamia, India, or even Asia) there can be no question that grappling must certainly be the oldest codified tradition of self-defense.

Attesting to its ancient history are the remnants of stone carvings on the walls of the Beni Hassan Temple tombs near Egypt's River Nile. Characterizing virtually all of the known grappling techniques used in modern grappling, the Beni Hassan sculptures clearly demonstrate that this discipline was codified at least three millennium before the birth of Christ.

Qinna

As understood by the Chinese, grappling became a refined science, enhanced only by the twisting of bones, separating tendon away from it, locking or dislocation of joints, and the impacting or traumatizing of anatomically vulnerable areas. It is hypothesized that qinna, meaning "to catch or seize and hold or control," served as the very first form of self-defense in China, long before the development of quanfa. A compilation of preordained self-defense responses to habitual attack scenarios prevalent to that period of their creation, qinna embodies the principles of seizing and controlling an adversary without seriously injuring him unless absolutely necessary.

Understanding the principles of qinna as they apply to karate-do begins with building a foundation of basic technique and learning the proper application of force. The effectiveness of qinna depends largely on understanding the amount of force to apply, its direction, and the manner in which it is applied. Without a strong foundation upon which to support your qinna, it cannot be used effectively. This is one reason why so much emphasis is placed upon developing sound basics and understanding the yin/yang five-element theory, as the Chinese originators did.

Because qinna has always been an effective deterrent in thwarting and controlling attackers, it has served as a practical adjunct for peace officers at various levels of law enforcement for centuries. In the practice of quanfa, qinna represents the application principle for each technique of which the *hsing* is comprised. In toudi-jutsu (the Chinese-based self-defense disciplines once vigorously cultivated during Okinawa's old Ryukyu Kingdom), this practice came to be called bunkai-jutsu.

Modern Japanese karate-do has popularized special terms in an effort to isolate the specific components of bunkai-jutsu, for example: *tori-te* (*tuidi* in Okinawan *hogan*, to seize with one's hands); *kyusho-jutsu* (techniques for attacking vital points); *tegumi* (grappling hands); *kansetsu-waza* (the locking and dislocation of joints); *shime-waza* (techniques of strangulation); *atemi-waza* (techniques of impact); *gyakyu-waza* (counters); *newaza* (ground work); *nage-waza* (throwing and takedowns, etc.).

In essence, qinna brings together all the principles of physical subjugation cultivated throughout untold generations of practical experience, and probably at the cost of untold human lives. Qinna embraces the principles of twisting bones, locking joints, and separating tendons from the bone; seizing, manipulating, and striking nerve plexuses, arteries, and other anatomically vulnerable locations; strangulations; organ-piercing blows; rupturing veins and arteries (blood-gate attacks); grappling techniques; takedowns, throws, and break falls; counters; escapes; and combinations thereof.

In addition to our complex network of nerves, the human body consists of organs, bones, tendons, and collaterals that are irrigated by arteries and veins. A person's movement can be impaired if his bones, tendons, or collaterals have been seriously injured. Moreover, if the blood or air flow has been impaired, or if one is in enough pain, one will lose consciousness. Striking vital points simply means closing down the lines of communication by causing pain, or by cutting off the transportation routes of blood, air, or energy.

Organ-piercing blows intended to shock those organs not protected by the rib cage, and techniques intended to rupture veins or arteries, called blood-gate attacks, serve the same purpose.[8]

Qinna teaches one how to discourage an attacker by hurting, incapacitating, or killing. A Shaolin code of conduct that has been handed down from ancient times rationalizes one's self-defense actions thusly: "Avoid fighting at all costs; however, when no other choice is available, hurt rather than be hurt, maim rather than be maimed, kill rather than be killed."

The results of untold ordeals, each qinna principle was ingeniously contrived in an effort to neutralize an opponent's ability to attack. This may be effected through causing paralysis, interfering with the adversary's respiration, rendering the opposition unconscious (by way of a neurological "attack"), or the activation of a death-points.

The hallmark of any orthodox quanfa style is the characteristic of their animal *hsing* (form) and the interpretation of their qinna principle. Representing the original self-defense experience of a style's originator, the application of qinna techniques may vary from style to style, but their principles always remain the same. Influenced by those most responsible for passing on a tradition, the application methods often vary depending on the specialties of the style or its master. Fist strikes, finger thrusts, head-butts, knee attacks, and kicks (or combinations thereof) all serve to enhance the application principles of qinna.

Physical Aims of Kata

Kata is a metaphor . . . the actual hides behind the visible. If you have not experienced it, it is quite difficult to understand. On the surface, kata training strengthens bone and muscle, which helps to maximize biomechanics. This refers to developing optimum performance with the least amount of energy, and includes the ability to vibrate, torque, rotate, expand, and contract—the total summation of joint forces. One learns to build, contain, and release *qi* energy through regulating the breath and synchronizing it with the expansion and contraction of muscular activity. Kata is also an excellent way of oxygenating the body and cultivating *qi* energy that has a positive therapeutic effect upon the body, both internally and externally. In short, kata serves to develop a healthy body, fast reflexes, and strong movements, thus increasing one's ability to respond effectively to potentially dangerous encounters.

Discussing the significance of breathing and the principles of *qi* energy, Fujian white crane master Lin Guozhong used the terms swallowing, spitting, floating, and sinking the breath,[9] and body to describe the importance of inhalation, exhalation, rising up and dropping the body down to maximize defensive effectiveness.

Master Wu Bin of the China Wushu Research Institute in Beijing describes combative paradigms as vitally important in mobilizing the inner circulation of air flow so as to guide it to all extremities, thus synthesizing one's internal and external forces. Kata is also an excellent way to keep the body electrically charged and physically tuned. When executed correctly, kata should not overstrain one's muscles nor cause injury, but rather massage one's internal organs and invigorate the body. Kata has long served as a remarkable therapeutic exercise through which diligent practice ultimately strengthens the body and helps prevent disease.

The deepest physical benefits of kata include: the strengthening of bones, muscles, and tendons; regulating the neurologic system; promoting circulation; massaging the internal organs; and balancing hormone production. This is accomplished when our energy channels are fully opened and appropriate alignments are cultivated. That is why in rooted postures the back must be straight, shoulders rounded, chin pushed in, pelvis tilted up, feet firmly planted, and the body remain pliable, so that energy can be circulated unobstructedly.

Prolonged practice of kata improves concentration, coordination, and the functions of various organs. The controlled breathing techniques, vigorous twisting of the body, oscillation of limbs, and the contractions and expansion of the muscles unimpedes *jingluo* (blood and lymphatic vessels) and improves the functions of the skeletal and muscular structures, as well as the digestive system. Hence, kata is an excellent adjunct for physical training as it provides curative effects for such chronic diseases as neurasthenia, high blood pressure, enterogastritis, heart trouble, tuberculosis, arthritis, diabetes, emissions, and piles.

Generally speaking, many of us impair our internal energy pathways through poor diet, obesity, smoking, inactivity, and indiscreet lifestyles. The unique group of alignments that orthodox kata cultivates opens the body's inner pathways, allowing the energy to flow spontaneously and hence nourish and invigorate the entire body. When the channels are purified energy flows freely, the neurological system is cleansed, and the internal organs are regulated.

An important point when considering kata should be to know that the techniques were never contrived to be used against a professional fighter in a rule-bound arena or even a warrior on the battlefield; rather, they were first developed to be used against a preoccupied aggressor who had virtually no understanding of the defensive principles use to counter the unwarranted act of aggression. In fact, to this day, self-defense applications work best against those who are completely unaware of the techniques being used to counter their assault.

Pregnant with a myriad of self-defense applications, kata needs to be studied deeply if we are to understand such defensive applications. A practice that has not become popular within karate-do's competitive element, and one that is only now forcing the international community of karate-do to reevaluate its understanding of the tradition.

Nonphysical Aims of Kata

In agreement with Uechi Kanbun (1877–1948), the founder of what has become the Uechi-ryu karate-do tradition, and a man who learned directly under the eminent tiger fist boxer of Fujian, Zhou Zhihe (1874–1926), Nagamine Shoshin said:

> Only through the relentless study of karate-do can one achieve the highest standards of inner beauty and strength. The fusing of the body and mind through karate-do is indescribably beautiful and spiritual. When totally absorbed in kata, one is brought into complete contact with the central core of one's being. It is there that the essence of karate-do is to be discovered.

Shito-ryu founder Mabuni Kenwa concluded that understanding karate-do's deepest meaning first meant transcending ego-related distractions and finding inner peace. In an abstract poem, Mabuni Sensei wrote:

> When the spirit of karate-do [written as *bu* for budo] is deeply embraced, it becomes the vehicle [described as a boat] by which one is ferried across the great void to enlightenment [that Master Mabuni described as an island].

Correctly studied, kata reveals both the physical and metaphysical precepts of karate-do. Best described through the abstract tenets of *shuhari,* Kinjo Hiroshi, a man characterized by Richard Kim as a walking encyclopedia of karate-do history, philosophy, and application, maintains that kata is karate-do, and karate-do is kata.

Shuhari (Obedience, Separation, Divergence)

Shuhari can be described as the three phases of transition—from beginner to master. The term *shu* literally means to protect or maintain, and represents "learning from tradition." This is the way the chain of tradition is perpetuated and passed on. This initial stage of training is an indispensable rung on the infinite ladder of growth and development within karate-do. There are no time limits for each of the three stages, and transition from one level to the next is neither simple nor immediate. Rather, levels tend to overlap each other in the transitional phase, which allows for a gradual withdrawal from one level, and a subtle entry into the next.

Secondary conditioning takes one beyond the boundaries of physical training and away from the tyranny of worldly delusion, the preoccupation of materialism and other ego-related distractions.

Ha literally means "to detach," and refers to breaking free from the chains of tradition. However, often misunderstood, it does not mean to depart from that which has given one strength, but rather represents a transitional phase from which a person emerges strengthened through the power of introspection.

Described as exploring the "world within," kata and protracted introspection become the focal point through which the supreme power of one's mind is first realized. Having a profound affect upon every aspect of one's life and understanding of karate-do, daily training, as with life itself, takes on a completely new meaning, as one continues a relentless pursuit to the next phase of mastery.

Ri is the final stage of transition and literally means to "go beyond" or "transcend." This is what is commonly referred to as enlightenment or spiritual emancipation. Daoists call it becoming one with the source, but is probably better described as unrestricted realization.

Continuing on the journey without distance through the world within, one is absorbed in its abyss, so much so that the intermittent flashes of penetrating wisdom become more frequent before one emerges reborn. Those who fail to make this inward journey remain forever unfamiliar with the true essence of karate-do and the self.

For the most part, this denotes the doctrine of *shuhari* that, in Zen, is often referred to as completing the circle or attaining a primordial state. Although its symbol is an empty circle, it is not void of meaning for those who stand within it, as it aims to bring one back into harmony with nature. The *shuhari* precept knows no time barrier.

More on Kata

To a beginner of karate-do, kata is the vehicle by which the central principles of self-defense are first learned. If there is anything else to be discovered beyond that, it is something that manifests itself after intense study and thousands upon thousands of repetitions; a practice that compels one to turn their attention inward. Miyamoto Musashi, a well-know samurai warrior of feudal Japan, when describing kata ritual, once wrote these provocative words, "Senjitsu no keiko tan to ii, Banjitsu no keiko rento yu" (One thousand days to forge the spirit, ten thousand to polish it).

Wise teachers often warn that when the spirit of repetition is not properly cultivated or, even worse, lost, the kata ritual becomes uneventful, even boring. It is said that there can be no limit placed upon kata training, philosophical assimilation, and protracted introspection.

Consumed within and by the kata, impermeable layers of silence shield one from both external and internal distractions. Inner confusion gradually dissolves until it no longer exists at all. Regulating the flow of air from within the body, and synchronizing it with the execution of each physical contraction, kata become a powerful vehicle of introspection through which external performance and internal thought correspond harmoniously. Internal and external disturbances fade away into a muffled roar until they are no more disturbing than the distant sound of rolling thunder.

Captured by the essence of introspection, personal concessions, diligent training, and philosophical assimilation establish an inner balance. Through this balance an immunity against life's trivial distractions is, in the fullness of time, established. So much so that detachment from illusion becomes easier and quicker. Breath is the gateway between the body and the mind, between the physical and the spiritual. In this light, kata becomes karate-do's central vehicle, like meditation in motion. Training becomes as much mental as it is physical.

Beyond exhaustion, despite aching muscles, we have all experienced a peacefulness flowing quietly within the brutality of karate-do. It is through this tranquillity that our pursuit of fulfillment is realized.

There are no superfluous movements in the orthodox karate-do paradigms. Each and every movements represents a specific principle that corresponds to its defensive application. Practicing kata, one's performance is enhanced if the *karateka* can actually visualize the physical application to which each technique applies, hence employing varying degrees of rhythm, power, and focus, Knowing this, we can better understand what Master Kinjo Hiroshi meant when he said: "the performance of kata reveals one's understanding of it."

Within Okinawa, up until the turn of this century, most (if not all) local disciplines revolved around only one or two kata. However, during Itosu Anko's era, this tradition changed due largely to the introduction and popularity of Toudi-jutsu (the name then used) within the school system. Later, when Toudi-jutsu was taken to the Japanese mainland, group instruction, school clubs, and the competitive format completely revolutionized the practice of kata and the study of karate-do.

Curiosity within the mainland about Toudi-jutsu prior to the turn of this century first surfaced from the attention it gained when the Imperial army considered its value as an adjunct to physical training. Impressed by the physical conditioning of several Okinawan conscripts during their medical examinations in 1891,[10] the army ultimately abandoned its interest in pursuing Toudi-jutsu because of unsafe training methods, poor organization, the great length of time it took to gain proficiency, and (ironically enough) the aggressiveness it fostered. However, that was not before a local campaign surfaced in an effort to modernize its practice. The movement, headed by Itosu Anko (1832–1915), was ultimately successful when Toudi-jutsu became a part of the physical education curriculum of Okinawa's school system at the turn of the century. In linking the past to the present, Itosu's crusade to modernize karate-do resulted in fundamentally revising its purpose and practice.

Beyond Itosu's letter of 1908, there is little testimony to support (or deny) allegations that Toudi-jutsu was developed in an effort to better prepare draftees for military service. Notwithstanding, Toudi-jutsu was ultimately introduced into Okinawa's school system under the pretense that young men with healthy bodies and good moral character were more productive in modern Japanese society.

With Master Itosu removing much of what was then considered "too dangerous" for schoolchildren, the emphasis shifted from a self-defense art to a cultural recreation for physical fitness that underscored the value of group kata (forms) practice, and neglected its *bunkai* (application). Ignoring the spiritual foundation upon which karate-do rested and not teaching the hidden self-defense applications (to disable, maim, or even kill, by traumatizing anatomically vulnerable areas), the old discipline became obscured and a new tradition evolved. Without its spiritual platform and ignoring the application of the kata, these geometrical paradigms became exercises for health and fitness during Itosu Anko's generation.

This period of radical transition represented the termination of a secret self-defense art and the birth of a unique recreational phenomenon. This phenomenon was introduced to the mainland where it ultimately conformed to the forces of Japanese-ness, thereby blossoming into a remarkable cultural recreational cultural discipline.

Compared to those mother paradigms of Chinese quanfa, the traditional kata of Japanese karate-do are noticeably different. However, without understanding how cultural forces affect the growth and direction of phenomena, it is perplexing at best to actually conceive the connection between Japanese karate-do and its progenitor, quanfa.

Understanding the social matrix from whence it evolved, we can more easily understand how Japan's inflexible and ritualistic society transformed these Chinese traditions once cultivated in old Okinawa. An old Japanese *kotowaza* (proverb) aptly describes how things or people that are "different" (that is, not in balance with *wa*) either ultimately conform or are methodically thwarted by Japan's omnipotent cultural forces: *Deru kugi wah utareru*—a protruding nail ultimately gets hammered down.

As I have mentioned earlier, there are various styles of Japanese karate-do, as each generation has produced innovators who have found reason to reinterpret karate-do's principles. However, if one looked deep enough, it would soon become apparent that the principles upon which that combative subjugation rest are universal.

In his illuminating dissertation on the evolution of Zen Buddhism and its effects upon Japanese culture, Suzuki Kakuzen Sensei[11] (at the Japan Budo University in 1990) aptly described how variations in human behavior (personality/attitude) were responsible for the advent of Zen's various sects.

Comparing his dissertation to karate-do's myriad of eclectic interpretations, it is easy to arrive at the same conclusion: The style is directly proportional to the experience, personality, and nature of its originator and/or those persons most responsible for its transmission. There is only one message, maintained Suzuki, but many ways of teaching it. A popular *kotowaza* used by men of budo in Japan reads: "Many paths lead up a mountain, but only one moon can be seen by those who achieve its summit." The principles upon which self-defense rest never vary, and it is those principles that we should strive to master.

Having been introduced to the mainland, the kata of Okinawa Toudi-jutsu, as with other ritualized Japanese disciplines, evolved into elegant but fixed traditions, beautiful in their simplicity. Compared to the complexities of Chinese quanfa, the *hsing,* as with other facets of Chinese society, remained abundant yet enigmatic.

Karate-do's Roots

Numerous Chinese *hsing* were introduced to Okinawa. Indeed, hundreds of Chinese forms may have haphazardly made their way to the tiny island kingdom over many generations. However, all that remains now of those original paradigms are approximately fifty, perpetuated in more than a dozen different self-defense traditions. Influenced by various cultural and individual factors, kata is a distinct collection of hallmarks that pertain to certain styles.

Bound by an iron-clad ritual of secrecy, the hidden self-defense applications of any style have always been handed down through oral tradition. Taking years of meticulous study, it is no wonder that its practice, compared to tournament fighting, became overshadowed and ultimately obscured.

The Magnitude of Kata

If we were to consider the myriad of self-defense-related phenomena to which a single kata applies, it would become readily apparent why kata is, in itself, an entire tradition. This is why the old masters of orthodox karate-do once advocated the mastery of one or two kata as opposed to the pointless, but popular, accumulation of many.

In addition to the seizing, holding, grappling, throwing, jointlocking, dislocating, strangling, and traumatizing techniques that are present within the kata, let us also consider some of the other principles with which the kata is concerned:

- *yoi no kishin* (mental preparation)
- *inyo* (yin/yang—understanding the magnitude of cause and effect)
- *go no sen, sen no sen,* and *sen* (the three aspects of defensive initiative)
- *maai* (understanding engagement distance and how to utilize *ma*—the space or interval established through body-change) and *tai sabaki* (the principles of balance and leading control)
- *tai no shinshuku* (expansion and contraction, gyration, and body mechanics)
- *chikara no kyojaku* (the proper amount of power for each technique)
- *kiai-jutsu* (the gathering and releasing of *ki* or *qi*)
- *waza no kankyu* (the speed and rhythm of technique)
- *ju no ri* (the principle of resiliency, and the willingness to bend in the wind of adversity)
- *kokyu* (synchronizing the breath as it pertains to the expansion and contraction of muscular activity)
- *bunkai* (understanding the defensive themes and application of technique)

- *zanshin* (mental alertness and continued domination before and after the fact)
- *seishi o choetsu* (transcending the thoughts of life and death)

Through understanding the magnitude of kata, especially when it is combined with spiritual doctrines, it becomes perfectly clear how a single paradigm (kata) can represent an entire fighting tradition. Once a student comes to grips with the gravity that each kata represents, their personal training will take on new direction and more meaningful dimension. Moreover, by genuinely embracing the precepts upon which karate-do rest, one is assured that its social ramifications will permeate the character of its user—hence, the value and direction of one's life in general is profoundly enhanced.

The Value of Karate-do in Modern Times

To be the very best one can ever be, regardless of whether or not it is in fighting, sports, business, or just life, requires indescribable resolve and inner strength. Transcending the barriers of the ordinary, such indomitable fortitude is never made possible without first making enormous personal sacrifices—a prerequisite to which any combat veteran, athletic champion, or successful businessperson can attest.

Through the virtues of karate-do one comes face-to-face with one's weaknesses, and it is through these virtues that weaknesses are turned into strengths, and strengths into even greater strengths, thus the tradition fulfills its purpose. Indomitable fortitude insulates us against the powerful forces of resistance, and provides the resilience to withstand personal failure.

A mind tempered in the tradition of karate-do will remain impervious to worldly delusion, while illuminating the darkness of selfishness and ignorance. As with the samurai warrior undaunted in the face of fear, preparation, patience, and humility is ninety percent of fighting, winning, and living. With greater control over our minds, or the world within, we can have greater control over our body, life, and the outside or physical world. It is by putting this power and knowledge to work every day that our lives are enriched and fulfilled in ways we never thought possible.

Those of you who are familiar with the power of combining physical training with methodical introspection can readily testify to the self-conquests made possible through karate-do. However, we in the West are a society of people who were first introduced to karate-do as a practical form of self-defense and a demanding but rewarding competitive recreation.

That its metaphysical significance remains unknown and the subject of intense curiosity in the Western world lends importance to the provocative words of Frenchman Henri Poincaré (1854–1912). A mathematician and philosopher of science, Poincaré, in 1905, wrote (in his book *Hypothesis of Science*) that "Science is built upon facts much in the same way that a house is erected from bricks, but that the mere collection of facts was no more a science than a pile of bricks a house." So, too, in this way is karate-do a science that, like any other science whose foundation has been fractured, abused, or removed altogether, is reduced in substance, taking on the characteristics of its new circumstances.

The foundation to which I refer is the training of one's mind. It is the very foundation upon which our predecessors, men such as Funakoshi Gichin, Motobu Choki, Miyagi Chojun, and Mabuni Kenwa placed so much emphasis.

Funakoshi Gichin described karate-do as an intangible vehicle through which inner discovery provoked a deeper understanding of the self, of life, and the world in which one dwells. Concerning the kara of karate-do, he also wrote: "Just as a valley can carry a resounding voice, so, too, must the person who follows karate-do make himself void or empty by transcending self-centeredness and greed. Make yourself empty within, but upright without. This is the real meaning of the kara of karate-do." The great master maintained that the ultimate aim of karate-do lies neither in victory nor defeat, but rather in the perfection of one's moral character.

Motobu Choki, a principal authority on Toudi-jutsu and a most controversial figure and celebrated fighter wrote, in 1927, that in seeking to understand the essence of karate-do we must search beyond the immediate results of physical training. We must not place too much emphasis on competition or record-breaking, he said, but seek wisdom through self-knowledge and humility.

Japanese Culture and Ritual

In many ways, karate-do is a miniature representation of Japanese society. Therefore, studying the pensive culture and provocative language from whence it came can also better help to deepen one's understanding of the art. Based on feudal customs, inflexible ideology, and profound spiritual conviction, modern Japan is a country rich in cultural heritage, but also a society that remains bound by ancient ritual.

For the most part, Japanese are disciplined and idealistic people. A microcosm of the austere society from whence it evolved, budo is also idealistic and disciplined. Ritual is the platform upon which karate-do is taught, and it is through the ritual that one's attention is ultimately turned inward, to where a lifelong journey for spiritual harmony is pursued. In this light, kata becomes the central vehicle for karate-do, and training becomes as much mental as it is physical. However, it is necessary to balance this ritual with philosophy and introspection before the light inside each of us can ever be turned on.

American anthropologist Dr. Stephen Fabian, in his preliminary analysis of methodology, described ju-jutsu as a miniature representation of Japanese culture and society. In this case, I believe that Dr. Fabian's use of the word *ju-jutsu* can and does represent Japanese budo in general, of which karate-do is a part. Drawing upon Fabian's analysis we can easily observe how the same principles apply to karate-do. Dr. Fabian wrote:

> As an outgrowth of the warrior ethos of pre-Meiji (before 1868) Japan, ju-jutsu is in many ways a microcosm of Japanese culture and society. It is more than a mere reflection of its setting, however; its practitioners dynamically interact with the socio-cultural environment of which they are an integral (if today but a small) part, and by doing so reinforce certain socio-cultural attributes.[12]

The combative principle of *ju,* or pliability, is also a precept found in general application throughout Japanese society, one where direct confrontation—and occasionally even contact—between interacting parties is avoided as much as possible. The principle of *wa* (or group harmony) in Japanese society, as in budo, is of the utmost importance. It is an attitude that, to varying degrees, is customarily practiced in all aspects of Japanese society. *Wa* can be described as the interrupted display of a readiness to sacrifice one's personal interests for the sake of communal tranquillity.[13]

Fabian continued his analysis by describing another set of related concepts observable within both Japanese society and budo. He described the *tatemae/honne* and *omote/ura* precepts by drawing upon Hall and Hall's study,[14] which states that *tatemae* is that which is openly presented, while *honne* remains the innermost feeling. Similarly, *omote* and *ura* are virtually synonymous with the *tatemae/honne* principles. For example, *omote* means the front, the face, or the image one presents, while *ura* refers to the back or that which cannot be seen—in other words, the hidden or concealed thought, feeling, emotion. These principles are observed within kata, where what is presented on the surface is not always what is truly intended.

A myriad of comparative sociocultural principles permeate the Japanese combative disciplines, and are worthy of our attention. However, while an entire analysis might better illuminate the magnitude of that study, this lecture is geared only to draw your attention to its existence.

In Western society we often measure the degree of our success or happiness by how much we possess. It is deeply ingrained in Japanese culture that true success and happiness is not necessarily found in acquiring more but, rather, learning to appreciate less. Indicative of what the Japanese call *mu* (nothingness, the void), this is a precept that permeates not only Japanese culture but karate-do and all the fighting traditions as well.

The Japanese believe that if one is able to go beyond ego-related distractions, the need for physical violence can be reduced entirely to chance. Basically speaking, it is ego that gets people into trouble. Karate-do (the way of karate) like other kinds of Japanese budo, is a conduit through which Japanese culture is also funneled. People who have mastered karate-do respect the principle of *wa* and find sincere personal reward cultivating both inner and outer harmony.

This is a concept rarely observed in Western culture, but one that represents a cornerstone of Japanese society. When one cannot get beyond the immediate results of physical training, karate-do remains purely a recreational pursuit. Captured by the essence of introspection, karate-do becomes a fascinating vehicle of inner exploration through which untold personal reward is possible. Those of you familiar with the power of combining physical discipline, philosophical research, and meditation can readily testify to the self-conquests made possible through karate-do.

Cultural differences, which have traditionally divided the East and the West, have made the understanding of oriental philosophy appear somewhat bewildering, if not totally confusing, to the Western mind. However, during an era when so many of us are now seeking ways to transcend the stress-related sickness of today's fast-paced society, the introspective traditions of the East, like karate-do, offer deeply rewarding alternatives. Teaching us how to get back to nature, so to speak, karate-do is one hundred percent holistic.

Some examples of this cultural essence can be found in the translated publications of Muso Soseki's *ni sente nashi* precept, Tsukahara Bokuden's *Spirit of the Immovable Mind,* Yamamoto Tsunemoto's *Hagakure,* Takuan Soho's *Unfettered Mind,* Miyamoto Musashi's *Book of the Five Rings,* and Yamaoka Tesshu's *Sword of No Sword,* to name but a few of the more popular ones. Reading these works will help enthusiasts better understand the Japanese mind, as well as affect the karateka development. However, in having said that, my own experience tells me that even learning needs to be balanced by understanding the science of politics in the martial arts as well. Hence, Machiavelli's *The Prince* should also be required reading.

Notwithstanding, personal research is vitally important to the growth and maturity of each and every one who studies karate-do, regardless of how skeptical we may at first feel. The research process is equally as important as is the end result, and I caution anybody who embarks upon such an adventure to understand this.

While it is fine to focus upon the rewards of success rather than the penalties of failure, it is critical not to lose sight of the importance of daily effort. Quite often we are so preoccupied by the ends to which our choices would be a means, that we rarely, if ever, pay attention to the causes of which our choices may be an effect.

The results of one's research usually holds more personal value when interest develops from attraction rather than promotion. In short, it is better to find out on your own how valuable research can be than to have someone else telling you how great it is. With one's attention drawn inward, the prolonged physical discipline of karate-do has a way of influencing the mind. It is in that regard that a karate-do student begins to recognize the depth of his or her tradition.

However, it usually takes quite some time and effort to begin to understand that there is something beyond the immediate results of physical training worthy of one's undivided attention. One must make sacrifices and work diligently to learn, for what can one ever discover if one is not first willing to explore. Only a fool takes no pleasure in understanding.

Exercising the Mind

Understanding the significance of karate-do as a path upon which its followers may discover the source of all human misery, and how to transcend its powerful forces, is to understand the spiritual foundation upon which budo rests. This is what is meant by the *do* (the "way") of karate-do. Lest we be burdened by the politics of religion, does it not seem more advantageous to simply honor the principles of spiritualism than to argue over which god is better?

There is no god nor devil; heaven and hell exist only in the mind. Such blasphemous words bring about confusion in the minds of people holier-than-thou. In 1927, Sigmund Freud, in *The Future of an Illusion,* wrote: "The truths contained in religious doctrines are, after all, so distorted and systematically disguised, that the mass of humanity cannot recognize them as truth."[15]

The ancient Hindu Vedas[16] tell us that "Truth is but one, yet the sages speak of it by many names," while an ancient Chinese proverb posits: "There are many paths which lead up a mountain, however, there is but one moon to be seen by those who achieve its summit."

From the myths of ancient man came spiritual rituals through which future generations could discover and study the life-enhancing ways of those who had already made the journey. Whether presented in the vast, almost oceanic images of the Orient, in the vigorous narratives of the Greeks, or in the majestic legends of the Bible, various traditions described a separation from society, an inward penetration to the source of power, and a life-enhancing return. And while the passage of this journey may be outward, in essence it is inward, into the center of our own existence. There, obscure resistance is finally overcome as we experience a marvelous expansion of our powers, a vivid renewal of life.

In karate-do, a disciple learns that self-mastery can only be accomplished by detachment and transfiguration. Fundamentally, this means transferring one's attention from the external world to the internal, from the macrocosm to the microcosm. It is a retreat from the quiet desperations of the material world to the tranquil realm of the world within in an effort to resurface free from the bondage of egotism.

Cultural anthropologist Joseph Campbell told us that throughout the inhabited world and under every circumstance myths have flourished; they have been the living inspiration for whatever else may have appeared out of the activities of the human body and mind. It would not be too much to say that myth is the secret opening through which the inexhaustible energies of the cosmos pour into the human cultural manifestation. Religion, philosophy, the arts, the social forms of primitive and historic man, prime discoveries in science and technology, the very dreams that blister sleep, boil up from the basic, magic ring of myth.[17]

In 1953 (in the foreword to Eugene Herrigal's *Zen in the Art of Archery*), the eminent Zen scholar Suzuki Daisetsu, in describing the correlation between spiritualism and the Japanese fighting traditions, wrote, "*budo,* as studied in Japan, is not pursued for its utilitarian purposes, nor purely for its aesthetic enjoyment, but is meant to train the mind; indeed, to bring the mind into contact with the ultimate reality."

Although an entire dissertation might better illuminate the power of "human thought," can you imagine, if one internalized one's training to equally balance their physical conditioning, what results it would have upon mind control and the art of thinking? In fact, it would be no understatement to imply that the source of all human power begins in thought, and that it is in the actual application of our thoughts that the condition conducive to growth and harmony (attitude) is created.

It is only through cultivating our spiritual nature that our faith, courage, and enthusiasm brings forth the abundant rewards of accomplishment. Our spiritual nature can only be cultivated by "doing"; we can only get as much as we give, we can only reap that which we sow. In fact, the law of growth depends entirely upon reciprocal action: We receive only as we give. Cultivating our spiritual nature begins with mastering a ritual of introspection and physical stillness long before its benefits can be put into practice.

With our attention drawn inward our thoughts are focused until the mind attracts the conditions necessary for their fulfillment. Concentration must become so intense that you identify with the object of your thought(s) and are thus conscious of nothing else. Ultimately, thought is transmuted into character (we are what we think) and it is that character that is the magnet which creates the individual's environment. Through developing our powers of perception, wisdom, intuition, and sagacity, our concentration intensifies. We need only to recognize the omnipotence of our spiritual nature, and the desire to become the recipient of its beneficial effects.

However, to exercise the mind, one must understand the law of cause and effect; causation depends entirely upon polarity: a circuit must be formed, the universe is the positive side of the battery of life; the individual is the negative; and thought forms the circuit.

Knowledge of this power provides the courage to dare and the faith to accomplish. The degree of success with which anyone will ever meet depends entirely upon the extent to which one realizes that the infinite cannot be changed but must be cooperated with. A change of thought means a change in conditions. The results of a harmonious mental attitude (the ultimate aim of karate-do) brings forth harmonious conditions in life. Selfish thoughts contain the germs of contamination. One's ability to appropriate that which one requires for growth from each of life's experiences determines the degree of harmony that we will attain. Obstacles are necessary for one's wisdom and spiritual growth.

Our ability to think is the ability to act and bring what we think into manifestation for the benefit of ourselves and others. What we do depends upon what we are, and what we are depends upon what we think. Success or failure is determined more or less by one's lifestyle. One's lifestyle is dominated by one's attitude. One's attitude depends entirely upon one's thoughts, underscored by the expression "we are nothing more than the sum total of our daily thoughts and decisions." Therefore, a person is what a person thinks. How a person speaks and behaves is, in essence, what that person thinks. Subsequently, thinking is crucial to being. This is true because one must *be* before one can *do,* and one can *do* only to the extent that one *is,* and what one *is* depends entirely upon what one *thinks.*[18]

We cannot express powers we do not possess. We must discover the power within and learn how to use that power in order to strengthen and enhance the outer or physical world. Karate-do is an art that teaches this technique. It teaches that the source of human weakness is internal, not external, hence the journey must always be inward, not outward. Understanding that the real enemy lies within is to know that it is there where all battles should be fought and won, before its benefit can ever be used in daily life.

Although the process is protracted, it is also quite unique and can, no doubt, change one's life and lifestyle if one so desires. There is an entire system to be learned that entails a series of mental exercises to be performed in methodical order.

The Technique

Let me introduce you to the preliminary technique used in karate-do through the following outline, albeit somewhat brief. I hope that you will optimistically embrace its value and consider seeking its further wisdom. Embracing this doctrine should occur from resolve, and not simply because someone told you how great it is. If you have remained unsuccessful in your quest to transcend the boundaries of physical training, or not yet discovered that there is something of enormous value beyond kicking and punching, perhaps you may be attracted to the methodical introspection that permeates karate-do, the art form.

Each day, upon waking and prior to sleep, find a place where you can sit comfortably and undisturbed for up to thirty minutes. Introspection is about becoming relaxed, finding inner quiet and harmony. It is about separating yourself from everything else around you, and setting your mind as free as a bird soaring in the sky. Achieving this condition allows one to identify and transcend personal weaknesses, a prerequisite for honesty, and a methodical practice. An unusual but not a difficult practice, karate-do teaches that the passage to understanding self-discovery lies on the middle path between both extremes. To achieve this understanding, karate-do employs both static and moving forms (kata) of meditation.

Introductory preparation for static training consists of sitting comfortably in a perpendicular posture (a chair will do nicely). Although your spine is upright, you remain relaxed, with your hands resting together in your lap and your eyes closed. Do not worry about what to think, and do not concern yourself with chanting exotic mantras. Simply allow your mind to digress freely while you breath quietly and deeply. Inhale through the nose and exhale through the mouth. This technique must be supported by a posture that allows unimpeded diaphragmatic movement, and although this may seem to be a rather simple request, you may very well have great difficulty finding the patience to perform even such a fundamental exercise for more than just a few minutes.

However, be sure that the benefits will undoubtedly manifest themselves within a few short weeks of embarking upon regular practice. The two main points to remember are: (1) regular exercise and mental training must work in harmony with each other in preparation for the next step; and (2) patience is a virtue, and I would encourage you to balance your physical and mental training with philosophical assimilation through reading the ancient documents left to us by our predecessors.

Conclusion

Karate-do teaches one to embrace the moment—to live in harmony with nature and our fellow man. It teaches one to understand one's own deep mystery, and while the metaphysical principles upon which karate-do rest are ancient, knowing their value is to understand how to apply them to the contemporary lifestyle in which we live, the relationships we share, and the community in which we dwell.

What would you say to those who believe that philosophy, introspection, and spirituality have no part in karate-do? You would have to conclude that they have yet to understand the essence of this profound tradition. We are so engaged in doing things to achieve purpose of outer value that we forget inner value, the rapture associated with being alive.

Taught as an art form, karate-do helps its learners discover a message that transcends punching and kicking, winning or losing. Rituals help explain life's goals, the problems one will face along the way, how to overcome them, and what to expect, ultimately. Karate-do teaches that the answer defeating the bondage of egotism is within all of us.

The ancient masters' spiritual teachings live on within the legacy of karate-do, and are cultivated in patience and humility. Humility builds strength from weakness and is the product of austerity (*shugyo* in Japanese), and it is through patience and humility that karate-do's innermost value is attained. It is also in patience and humility that karate-do's rewards are best enjoyed.

Understanding that karate-do is a deeply personal pursuit that affects each of us in different ways, how can mastery ever be found within anything as shallow as physical prowess, race, orthodoxy of style, or lineage. It can only be in the sincere acceptance and genuine application of those virtues, values, and principles upon which karate-do rests that mastery without delusion can emerge. This message has made a significant impact on the pioneers of this ancient fraternity, and it is this message that has been perpetuated.

Bushi Matsumura Chikudoun Pechin Sokon (c. 1809–1901), the Miyamoto Musashi of the Ryukyu Kingdom, was responsible for introducing the teaching principles of Jigen-ryu ken-jutsu to the Chinese quanfa discipline of which he was an expert. Considered within karate-do history as the principal authority on the self-defense traditions that ascended the castle district of Shuri, he once wrote:

> To all those whose progress remains hampered by ego-related distractions let humility, the spiritual cornerstone upon which the fighting traditions rest, serve to remind you to place virtue ahead of vice, values ahead of vanity, and principles ahead of personalities.

Rather than gaining or acquiring excess baggage in life, karate-do teaches us to remove useless and ego-related distractions. Instead of always striving to acquire more and more, karate-do teaches one that genuine satisfaction can come from learning to appreciate less and less. Rather than only taking from karate-do, we must also consider putting back into that which has given us strength and power. Remember that all power and success has to do with putting knowledge into action through mastering the world within. Karate-do teaches us how to enhance our world without by accessing, cultivating, and mastering our world within.

How much we experience, but how little we truly learn. We understand many things but realize practically nothing. We hold many facts and opinions yet, in essence, know little about ourselves. Pretending will never change anything. How can one ever plan an escape without first realizing that one is imprisoned? One must pound and polish the human spirit until it is as strong and vibrant as a samurai sword. The secret of change is not to fight the old but rather to focus upon building the new. In the universe things are either expanding or contracting; the only thing constant in life is change.

Karate-do teaches that the source of human weakness is internal and not external; thus our journey must be inward not outward. Our responsibility, as students of karate-do, lest we neglect the essence of this profound discipline, is to foster this message. Metaphorically speaking, the sensei is like a lighthouse: He reveals the locations of the rocks; however, how one navigates those dangerous waters is entirely one's own concern. Karlfried Graf Durckhein once said, "When you're on a journey, and the end (goal) keeps getting further and further away, only then can you realize that the real end (goal) is, in fact, the journey itself." Karate-do teaches one to embrace the moment, to focus oneself upon the race rather than the finish line, in the pursuit not just the possession.

The only place to enjoy the rewards of karate-do is in the privacy of one's own thought. After years of traveling and seeking out the truth, I came to understand the old proverb "One need never leave the dojo to find that which one seeks. Look within to find the answers." When the teacher becomes the student, the master a beginner, and the end a beginning, the circle has been completed. T. S. Eliot once wrote: "We shall not cease from exploration, and at the end of all of our exploring, we will arrive where we first started and know the place for the first time."[1]

The passage of time, the change of seasons, the erosion of land, and the death of loved ones: The "way" of karate-do teaches those willing to learn that everything within the circle of life is seasonal, changing, dying, reborn. A microcosm of life, karate-do is but one path leading up the mountain; it teaches one to understand these changes, accept them, and live in harmony with them.

Our aging, the way we think, one's urges and sexuality, man's question about the universe, our necessity to know ourselves, and the need to find a reason for existence and acceptance of (our own) death will always need meticulous examination and action. Because these questions will always exist, there will always be the need for a tradition that has the answers. Karate-do, is one such tradition: a tradition that can only be brought to life by teaching its participants to look inward in an effort to discover the truth. This is the magnitude of karate-do.

In discovering that which lies beyond the immediate results of physical training, we have learned about the art and spirit of karate-do. It is something that each of you have inside but seek to better understand. Like the karate-do enthusiasts who have walked before us, we, too, need to establish a symbiosis with karate-do so that our lives are just as much a product of the art as the art is a product of our lives. However, a provocative question that remains unanswered invites each of us to seriously consider not only what one can get by continually taking from this humble tradition, but rather, as responsible enthusiasts concerned with its future direction, what one can put back into karate-do . . . the art and way of karate.

Itosu Anko told us that "karate strives to build character, improve human behavior, and encourage modesty; however, it cannot guarantee it."

Through studying the past we are brought that much closer to understanding the present. Research of this nature is critical if we are ever to transcend the limitations of physical training, and master the self.

I sincerely hope that my lengthy presentation has, if even only in some small way, helped you to gain an alternative perception of karate-do, and in doing so brought you closer to that which you have yet to discover. If so, then I will have succeeded in accomplishing what I set out to do. Thank you.

Patrick McCarthy
Copenhagen, 1995

Notes and References

....

Part 1

1. Gongfu is a generic Chinese-Mandarin term denoting the various self-defense traditions that developed from either the Buddhist Shaolin Temple (i.e., Dragon, Leopard, Tiger, Crane, Snake) or the Daoist Wudang Temples (i.e., Taijiquan, Bagua, Xingyi); it generally means "accomplished work." There are two current, more specific Mandarin terms used that are fraught with political undertones: *wushu*, "war arts," is the accepted term in the People's Republic of China (PRC), or mainland China; Taiwan, or the Republic of China, uses the term *guoshu* (*kuo shu* in Wade-Giles romanization), or "national arts." A third common term, *quanfa*, "way of the fist," is rendered as kenpo in Japanese. In general, wushu refers to the modernized, very acrobatic styles of gongfu, whereas gongfu, quanfa, and guoshu refer to the more traditional civil self-defense forms. All Chinese-Mandarin terms are rendered in the Pinyin romanization system used in the PRC.

2. A generic Okinawan term used until December 1933 to describe the Chinese-based eclectic civil self-defense disciplines as they evolved in Okinawa.

3. Often mistakenly referred to as *shizoku*, the term *keimochi* is used to describe people with a chronicled lineage during Okinawa's Ryukyu

Kingdom period. *Shizoku* is a Meiji period Japanese term used to denote members of the former samurai class. *Mukei* (peasant class) refers to those Okinawans without a chronicled lineage.

4. This generation refers to the era in which Okinawa's two mainstream self-defense traditions, Nahadi, and Shuridi, were popularized by Higashionna Kanryo and Itosu Ankoh.

5. There are three versions regarding Sakugawa's birth and death dates: 1733–1815, 1762–1843, and 1744–1838.

6. Graham Noble, "Master Funakoshi's Karate," *Fighting Arts International Magazine,* Issue #61.

7. Chitose Tsuyoshi, the founder of Chitoryu karate-do and a student of Aragaki, reported his date of death as 1918.

8. "Karatedo Kyohan," English translation by Oshima Tsutumu (Kodansha International, 1973), p. 8.

9. Gima Shinkin and Fujiwara Ryozo, *Kindai Karatedo no Rekishio Kataru,* (Tokyo: Baseball Magazine, 1986), p. 34.

10. Nakaya Takao, *Karatedo, History and Philosophy* (Carrollton, Tex.: JSS Publishing Co., 1986), p. 38.

11. The Ochayagoten (literally, the great tea palace), in Shuri's Sakiyama district, was a beautiful garden area where the Sapposhi and other dignitaries would wait prior to their audience with the king.

12. *Nihon Budo Taikei,* vol. 8, chapter on Karatedo (Tokyo, 1982), p. 60.

13. *Karatedo,* Sozo Kabushikigaisha (Tokyo, 1978), p. 60–61.

14. Gima Shinkin (1896–1989) was born in Naha and first studied Toudi under Itosu and Yabu Kentsu. Before going to Tokyo, he served as the president of the Okinawa Teachers College Toudi club. He is perhaps best remembered as the young man from Tokyo Shoka University who assisted Funakoshi Gichin in Tokyo with his 1922 demonstration at the First National Athletic Exhibition and later at the Kodokan demonstration for Kano Jigoro

15. Ibid. p. 90. Kano was invited to Okinawa by the prefectural Judo Yudanshakai (Okinawa Prefecture Judo Black Belt Association) on all three occasions.

16. Kano's visit and the demonstration are described in the *FAJKO Karatedo Directory* (p. 86), as being held in 1927.

17. *Kindai Karatedo no Rekishio Kataru,* p. 270.

18. Ibid. p. 143.

19. "Kano Jigoro Taikei," 2nd ed., vol. 13, edited by the Kodokan, (Tokyo: Abe Osamu, 1994), pp. 107–108.

20. Ibid. p 77.

21. Ibid. p 86.
22. Fujiwara Ryozo, *FAJKO Karatedo Directory,* proofed by WUKO (Tokyo: Sozo Co. Ltd., 1979), p. 81.
23. Historian, author, and karatedo master Kinjo Hiroshi was born in Shuri, Okinawa, in 1919, and is a direct disciple of Hanashiro Chomo and Oshiro Chojo.
24. Dr. Yang Jwing-Ming, "Analysis of Shaolin Qin na," (Jamaica Plains, Mass.: 1991) YMAA Publication Center, p. 1.
25. Specifically Hanashiro Chomo and Yabu Kentsu, who were cited for their superb physical shape.
26. Translation by Patrick and Yuriko McCarthy (Yokohama: IRKRS, August 1994).
27. I believe that the term *Shorei* is an error made by Itosu when describing the Chinese soft-style fighting traditions of Wudang. This error most probably occurred when civil fighting was handed down by oral tradition in an iron-clad ritual of secrecy. Often there are mispronunciations when two different languages interface.
28. The Showa Period of Japanese history was from 1925 until 1989.
29. Uechi Kanbum had studied Tiger Boxing in China's Fujian Province directly under Master Zhou Zhihe (1874–1926).
30. Konishi Yasuhiro, "Karatedo Johatsuho," (Tokyo: 1933), p. 156–161.
31. According to Fujiwara Ryozo (*Kindai Karatedo no Rekishio Kataru,* p. 235), Mabuni often privately referred to his style as Mabuniryu. However, in selecting formally a name to represent his teachings, Gima Shinkin said that "Mabuni was far too modest to ever use his own name to publicly advertise his style."
32. Responsible for domestic law enforcement and related matters, pechin were mid-class civil servants during the old Ryukyu Kingdom: Two classes of pechin included the Satunushi (selected from Keimochi—people with a chronicled lineage) and Chikudoun (chosen from those commoners who had distinguished themselves). Sai and bo were standard issue for law enforcement officials in feudal Okinawa nearly a century before Tokugawa's Edo kasatsu (policemen of Japan's Edo period [1603–1968]).
33. Also known as Yamane no Chinen, the founder of Yamaneryu kobudo.
34. A teacher's certificate.
35. "The 1936 Meeting of the Masters" (an English translation of its minutes), Patrick and Yuriko McCarthy (Yokohama: IRKRS, 1994), p. 9.
36. *Shijitsu to Koden ni Yoru-Okinawa no Karate Sumo Meijin-den* (Tokyo: Shinjimbutsu Oraisha, June 10, 1986).

37. Regarded as a master fighter, Motobu Choki insisted that the scholar Funakoshi Gichin was an impostor whose karate, although elegant, was ineffective because he had no idea of its application. Motobu felt Funakoshi was able to deceive many because of his tricky behavior and eloquent explanations. This resulted in Motobu issuing a public challenge to Funakoshi. Irreconcilable rivals, Funakoshi described Motobu as a densely illiterate person and refused the challenge. Motobu compared Funakoshi to a shamisen (a three-stringed instrument) player— a lovely sound but hollow inside—and continued his character attack upon Funakoshi. On the other hand, every time Motobu's name was mentioned in the presence of Funakoshi, his face contorted in disgust, said Konishi Yasuhiro, who described their hatred for each other like that of a cat and a dog. (*Karate and His Life,* [Tokyo: Kaku Kozu, Ryobukai, 1993], pp. 13–15.)

38. Often mistakenly rendered as "jitsu" in the West, which means "day," as in ju-jitsu (which actually means "gentle day"), or even more amusingly "kyushojitsu" (meaning "vital point day")!

39. The *Bubishi* was first translated into English by this author and his wife, Yuriko, and is now available from Charles E. Tuttle Publishing Company.

40. *The History of Karate* (Naha: Hirugi Company, 1987), p. 212

41. The Tokyo Shudokan was established in 1930 by Okinawan karate master Toyama Kanken. Toyama Sensei had studied under such legendary masters as Itosu Ankoh, Higashionna Kanryo, Oshiro Chojo, and Chibana Choshin.

42. Sponsored by the *Ryukyu Shinposha* newspaper, company, this historic gathering—to discuss the using of the ideogram to describe the kara of karate-do, and the establishment of an organization through which to unify and standardize the discipline—was held in Okinawa on October 25, 1936, at Naha's Showa Kaikan (meeting hall) and hosted many of the island's most prominent authorities of karate. In attendance were Hanashiro Chomo, Kyan Chotoku, Motobu Choki (1871–1944), Chibana Choshin (1885–1969), Kiyoda Juhatsu, Miyagi Chojun, and Gusukuma Shimpan.

43. Mabuni Sensei used the term *goju* (hard and soft) to symbolize the unique features of his self-defense method: Hard (*go*) characterizes the material force of the human body, while softness (*ju*) represents the principle of pliability, the potential to yield in the winds of adversity, also a character trait aspired for.

Notes and References

Part 2

1. The Sapposhi [often called Sakuhoshi or Sappushi] were special envoys of China's emperor. They traveled to outer reaches of their lord's domains carrying important dispatches and returning with situational reports. Accompanied by an entourage of four hundred to five hundred people (occupational specialists, tradesmen, and security experts) and staying for about four to six months, the Sapposhi journeyed to the Ryukyu Kingdom more than twenty times in nearly five centuries; approximately once for every new king that came to power from the time of Bunei-O in 1404. China's Ming dynasty extended from 1368 until 1644.

2. Keimochi is an Okinawan term used to describe people with a chronicled history; people of position (they are often mistakenly referred to as Shizoku). The pechin (*peichin*) class were mid-level ranked subordinates of the Ryukyu king. Largely responsible for, but not limited to, civil administration and domestic law-enforcement, they served from 1509 until 1879: that period of time from when King Sho Shin imposed a class structure upon the gentry until the dynasty was finally abolished. Satunushi pechin were from the gentry where the Chikudoun Pechin were from among common people.

3. The Ryukyu Kingdom was militarily subjugated by the Satsuma Samurai in May of 1609.

4. The civil fighting traditions, not unlike Japan's combative disciplines, were fostered in an iron-clad ritual of secrecy after the Satsuma occupied Okinawa.

5. Born in Shuri (Okinawa) and having trained directly under Hanashiro Chomo, Kinjo Sensei was a principal authority responsible for the postwar revival of karate within the Dai Nippon Butokukai and is presently regarded as one of the tradition's most eminent masters and historians.

6. Conversations with Konishi Yasuhiro, the founder of the Shindo jinen ryu karate-jutsu tradition. Together with Ohtsuka Hironori, the founder of Wado ryu ju-jutsu kempo, Konishi was largely responsible for establishing the movement that revolutionized Toudijutsu.

7. Karel van Wolferen, in his book *The Enigma of Japanese Power* (London: MacMillan Ltd., 1989), describes the principle of *wa* as the uninterrupted display of a readiness to sacrifice one's personal interests for the sake of communal harmony.

8. Although the Dai Nippon Butokukai endorsed the new term *kara-te-doh* in December of 1933, it was not ratified in Okinawa until October of 1936.

9. At a special gathering held in October of 1936 at the Showa Kaikan in Naha, sponsored by Ota Chofu (editor of the *Ryukyu Shimpo Sha* newspaper), senior authorities like Kyan Chotoku, Hanashiro Chomo, Motobu Choki, Yabu Kentsu, and Miyagi Chojun, etc. agreed that the new generic term *karate-doh* (the way of karate), using the new prefix and suffix, should be accepted and used.

10. Kuninda is the native pronunciation for Naha's Kume village where, in 1392, Ming China established its own settlement after ratifying a liaison with Chuzan; the most powerful of the "three rival" principalities in the Ryukyu Kingdom.

11. Refers to the publication *Oshima Hikki* compiled by a seventeenth-century Confucian scholar named Tobe Ryoen from Kochi Prefecture in Shikoku. Petitioned to interview and record the testimony of those passengers and crew of a Ryukyuan "tribute ship" that, blown off course in a typhoon en route to Satsuma while transferring "treasure," drifted to Kochi in 1762, a provocative passage provides the first mention of Chinese kempo in the Ryukyu Kingdom. Describing a demonstration of Chinese martial arts, Shiohira Pechin, the official in charge of the voyage, recounted his recollection of Kusankun.

12. The Keicho period, in Japanese history, was from October 22, 1596, until July 13, 1615. Miyagi Sensei is referring to the Ryukyu Kingdom being subjugated by the Satsuma Samurai in 1609. Being completely disarmed it is believed that an alternative means of law enforcement and civil defense was cultivated in lieu of having no weapons.

13. Miyagi uses Toudi and kempo (quanfa) as generic terms both describing the same fighting tradition.

14. Both Chinese and Japanese folklore tells us that pre-nineteenth-century martial arts training (especially in the case of uchi-deshi, or live-in apprentice) was a severe ritual that often entailed years of rigorous drudgery in unrelated activities to establish loyalty and character before even the most elementary of techniques were ever taught.

15. The school year in Japan begins in April as opposed to September in the Western world.

16. The eleventh year of Busei was 1828. Busei was Japan's emperor from April 22, 1818, until December 10, 1830.

17. Toki and musubi, in Miyagi's explanation, represent an unfettered

mind and completing the circle of understanding: spiritual emancipation.

Part 3

1. Okinawan karate-do master Toyama Kanken established the Tokyo Shudokan in 1930. Toyama Sensei had studied under such legendary masters as Itosu Ankoh, Higashionna Kanryo, Oshiro Chojo, and Chibana Choshin.

2. Two Chinese ideograms (called *kanji* in Japanese) represent the term *karate-do:* the first ideogram means China or, to be more specific, China's Tang dynasty (A.D. 618–907), and later came to represent China itself. The second ideogram means hand. The first ideogram can be pronounced either tou or kara, while the second ideogram can be pronounced either *te* or *di.*

3. The Japan of 1936 was at its peak of militarism. Nationalism was widespread, and dissension with China ultimately led to the outbreak of war in July 1937.

4. *Hiragana* is one of two Japanese standard syllabi that represent the sound of Chinese ideograms but carries no inherent meaning. In other words, by looking at an ideogram one can immediately recognize its meaning whereas by reading the *hiragana* one cannot readily understand its original meaning.

5. By doing so, karate-do's relationship to China became obscured.

6. The suffix *do,* as in kendo, judo, and budo, means way, path, or road, and can even mean province. The same character is also pronounced dao in Mandarin, and is most notably used for the Daoist philosophy of Lao Zi, reputed author of the *Dao De Jing.* In the philosophical context adopted by the self-defense traditions, *do* means a way of life, a path one travels to improve oneself.

7. Gongfu (literally, ability) is a generic Chinese-Mandarin term denoting the various self-defense traditions that developed from either the Buddhist Shaolin Temple (i.e., dragon, leopard, tiger, crane, and snake styles) or the Daoist Wudang Temples (i.e., Taiji, bagua, and xingyi); it generally means "accomplished work." There are two current and more specific Mandarin terms used, fraught with political undertones: *wushu* (war arts) is the accepted term within the People's Republic of China (Mainland China) while Taiwan (the Republic of China) uses the term *guoshu* (*kuoshu* in Wade-Giles romanization), or "national arts."

A third common term, *quanfa,* "way of the first," is pronounced *kempo* in Japanese. In general, wushu refers to the modernized, acrobatic styles of gongfu, whereas gongfu, quanfa, and guoshu refer to the more traditional civil self-defense forms. All Chinese-Mandarin terms are rendered in the Pinyin romanization system used within the People's Republic of China.

8. Miyagi is referring to the way that the fundamental elements of Japanese swordsmanship (ken-jutsu) and grappling (ju-jutsu) were brought together to establish kendo and judo, respectively. The principles of several Chinese-based self-defense disciplines (cultivated during the old Ryukyu Kingdom period) were also ultimately codified in an effort to form an indigenous tradition.

9. Buwa is (presumably) a place in China.

Part 4

1. Primarily Fujian monk, crane, and tiger fist boxing.
2. Meaning martial arts, also referred to as bu-jutsu, the koryu, or classical combative disciplines of Japan's feudal samurai warrior.
3. Karel van Wolferen, *The Enigma of Japanese Power* (London: MacMillan Ltd., 1989), p.412.
4. A propaganda phrase, popular during Japan's escalating era of militarism.
5. Shushin and Kokutai represented diligence, regimentalism, conformism, the commitment to mass productivity, strict adherence to seniority, emperor worship, and lifetime loyalty to its precepts.
6. Itosu is regarded as the grandfather of modern karate. Bringing together several traditions, he made learning a safer and methodic practice, which surfaced under the name of Ryukyu kempo karate-jutsu.
7. Ogawa was a bureaucrat from the Kagoshima prefectural branch (Okinawa had once been under the jurisdiction of Kagoshima—the new name for Satsuma) of the Mombusho (Ministry of Education).
8. Corroborated by Funakoshi Gichin (1868–1957), in his 1956 publication entitled *Karatedo, My Way of Life* (English translation, Kodansha, 1975), p. 43. "The Imperial Navy's first Fleet under the command of Admiral Dewa and a small contingent spent a week at the dormitory of the Prefectural First Middle School receiving a grounding in Toudi-jutsu."
9. Found in several publications (*Informal Talks with Yasuhiro, Memories of Karate, Karate and His Life,* etc.) and corroborated by personal inter-

views with Konishi's son, Takehiro, in 1992 and 1993, at his residence in Tokyo.

10. "Ippon Shobu" literally means one-point contest, a concept that evolved from the "shinken shobu" of feudal Japan: a match where one fatal blow of the sword determined the outcome of a duel.

11. Regarded as the master fighter, Motobu Choki insisted that the scholar Funakoshi Gichin was an imposter whose karate, although elegant, was ineffective because he had no idea of its application; however, because of his tricky behavior and eloquent explanations, Motobu felt Funakoshi was able to deceive many. This resulted in Motobu issuing a public challenge to Funakoshi. Irreconcilable rivals, Funakoshi described Motobu as a densely illiterate person, and refused the proposal. Motobu compared Funakoshi to a samisen (guitar) player—a lovely sound but hollow inside—and continued his character attacks upon Funakoshi. On the other hand, every time Motobu's name was mentioned in the presence of Funakoshi, his face contorted in disgust, said Konishi Yasuhiro, who described their hatred for each other like that of a cat and dog. (*Karate and His Life* [Tokyo: Kaku Kozu, Ryobukai, 1993], pp. 13–15.)

12. In recognizing the need to distinguish the varying grades of proficiency, Kano Jigoro, the founder of judo, developed a value standard called the dan/kyu system; the kyu represented the varying levels of proficiency below the dan, or black belt, level.

13. In preparation for Kano Jigoro's monumental visit to Okinawa in January of 1927, the prefecture recommended using a name that might characterize Toudi-jutsu as a martial tradition more closely associated with Okinawa rather than the existing name, which accented its foreign origins. In doing so the terms *Shuri-te, Naha-te,* and *Tomari-te* (meaning the *te* disciplines that were native to Shuri, Naha and Tomari) were born.

14. The problem with this testimony is that Moriwasa, a member of the Imperial Household, did not become the *sosai* [general director] of the Butokukai in 1942.

Part 5

1. From Michael Maliszewski, Ph.D., "Meditative Religious Traditions of Fighting Arts & Martial Ways," *Journal of Asian Martial Arts,* vol 1, no. 3 (July 1992), pp. 35–36.

2. Quanfa is a Chinese Mandarin term denoting the various self-defense

Notes and References

traditions that surfaced from within the monastic sanctuary of the Buddhist Shaolin Temple. All Chinese terms have been rendered in the Pinyin romanization system.

3. *Kemochi* is an Okinawan term that refers to those with a chronicled lineage: aristocracy. A Meiji period Japanese term, *shizoku,* which describes members of the former samurai caste, is often mistakenly used to describe Okinawa's aristocracy. The opposite of *kemochi* is *mukai*—those without a chronicled lineage: commoners.

4. The pechin were mid-level subordinates during the old Ryukyu Kingdom. They served from 1509 to 1879, starting from when Shoshin-O imposed a class structure upon the gentry until the dynasty was abolished. The pechin officials were largely responsible for, but not limited to, varying degrees of civil administration and law enforcement. The pechin class was divided into satunushi and chikudoun. The satunushi were from *kemochi* while the chikudoun came from mukei.

5. Yazaki Takeo's *Social Changes and the City of Japan* (Tokyo: Japan Publications, 1968), p. 251, lists 1,240 peasant revolts on Japan's mainland during the 268 years from 1599 to the end of the Edo Period in 1867. Hence, it is not without reason that those misinformed might consider that a similar phenomenon took place in Okinawa's history. Okinawa, however, not without its own problems, has no history of such uprisings—a significant historical point corroborated by Takara Kurayoshi, curator of the Urazoe Municipal Library and regarded as an eminent authority in Ryukyu history.

6. Used by Sir Winston Churchill when describing Russia on October 1, 1939.

7. Climate and geography have always played an important role in shaping the infrastructure of any fighting style: As an example: Northern Chinese gongfu styles evolved in rugged country and under harsh climatic conditions versus Southern Chinese gongfu styles that evolved under less trying circumstances. Therefore, clothing, a person's physical structure, and his environment profoundly influenced the development of man's combative techniques.

8. Jin Yiming, *Wudang Quanshu Mijua* (The Secrets of Wudang Boxing), (China: 1928), pp. 33–57. English translation by this author and his wife (IRKRS, 1994).

9. Robert W. Smith, *Chinese Boxing: Masters and Methods* (Berkeley, Calif.: North Atlantic Books; 1974/1990), p. 93.

10. Specifically Hanashiro Chomo and Yabu Kentsu, who were cited for their superb physical shape due to Toudi-jutsu training.

11. An Aikido shihan and the head priest at the Enkakuji Temple in Kita Kamakura, where Funakoshi Gichin's monument "Karate ni Sente Nashi" is located, Suzuki sensei is a professor of religion and is in charge of the Zen Research Center at Komazawa University.
12. Hoplos, "Hontai Yoshin Ryu Ju Jutsu" ("A feudal based combative tradition") vol. 7, no. 2 (Winter issue, 1992), pp. 1–7.
13. Karel van Wolferen, *The Enigma of Japanese Power* (London: MacMillan Ltd., 1989), p. 412.
14. Edward T. Hall and Mildred Reed Hall, *Hidden Differences* (Garden City, N.Y.: Anchor Press/Doubleday, 1987), p. 61.
15. Joseph Campbell, *The Hero with a Thousand faces,* Bollingen Foundation, N.Y., (Princeton, N.J.: Princton University Press, 1949, 1973), Preface.
16. The most sacred writings of ancient Hinduism provide some of the world's earliest spiritual philosophy.
17. Campbell, *Hero with a Thousand Faces,* p. 3.
18. J.F. Fennell, *The MasterKey* (date and publisher unknown).

Conclusion

1. "Four Quartets, Little Gidding" by Thomas Stearns Eliot (1888–1965) written 1942.

ANCIENT OKINAWAN MARTIAL ARTS

Volume Two

KORYU UCHINADI